# Why The Conservative Mind Matters

*A Collaboration of Essays
with Bill Owens*

Why The Conservative Mind Matters
*Conservative Family Values:: A Biblical Perspective*

Copyright 2008 © Bill Owens
email: william.owens@bellsouth.net

Published by: Higher Standard Publishers
http://www.higherstandardpublishers.com
P.O. Box 1395 Fuquay Varina, NC 27526
800-791-5806

Cover Design: William Owens, Jr.
Inside Layout: David Owens

Owens, Bill.
Why The Conservative Mind Matters / Bill Owens
p. cm.
ISBN: 978-0-61523-230-0
1. Christianity --United States. 2. Christianity and politics -
United States.

Printed in the United States of America!

# Contents

Acknowledgments .......................................... 11
Foreword ...................................... 13


Bill Owens ........................................... 15

*I Am A Conservative Because...*

I Am a Conservative Because I Care About
  Scriptural Living, not Merely Scriptural Quotation ...... 17
I Am a Conservative Because I Care About Family
  Values Lived, not Merely Family Values Voiced .......... 18
I Am a Conservative Because I Care About Individual
  Choice, not Merely Public Conformity ...................... 19
I Am a Conservative Because I Care About Genuine
  Diversity, not Merely Group Membership .................. 21
I Am a Conservative Because I Care About Human
  Dignity, not Merely About Human Glory .................. 22
I Am a Conservative Because I was Raised in a
  God-fearing, Committed Family .............................. 24


J. Kenneth Blackwell ............................ 25

*The Conservative Movement: A Light in Dark Times*

The Fierce Urgency of Now ............................ 26
Moral Coherence and the Promise of America .............. 27
Advancing the Big Ideas .................................. 29
Dedication and Purposeful Action ........................ 31
Punching Holes in the Darkness ............................ 33

Tracy Brown .............................................................. 37

*THE BLACK CHURCH*
*Urban America's Voice of Conscience for Family Values*
Parental Guidance ........................................................ 40
Advocacy for "Life" ...................................................... 40
Advocacy for Marriage and Family ................................ 41
A National Plan for the Black Church ........................... 42

Dr. Paul Cameron ..................................................... 45
*Conservative Solutions To Sexual Injustice*
Society As A Gigantic Clinic ......................................... 47
The Problem of Too Few Children ................................ 50
Solutions: .................................................................... 52
Where Persuasion Is Insufficient ................................. 53
In Sum ......................................................................... 55
References .................................................................... 55

Charles Colson .......................................................... 59
*Why I am a Conservative*

William J. Federer ..................................................... 75
*Conserving the Freedom of Religion*

William F. High .......................................................... 95
*The Generous Life*

Eddward T. Holliday ................................................ 105
*Inspired Conservatism*

Pastor Andrew Jackson ............................................ 115
*Conservative Family Values: A Biblical Perspective*
Someone Might Ask: "Where's the proof?" .................... 117

## Dr. Alveda C. King with Elizabeth Stoner ......... 127
*Shedding the Labels and Boxes: Embracing the Truth*
First, Labels Stick ............................................. 130
Second, Labels Are Hard to Remove ............................ 130
Third, Patch, Move On And Heal ............................... 131

## James Linzey, D.D. ..................................... 135
*The Ten Commandments as the*
*Root of American Culture*
Moral Leadership ............................................. 148
Bibliography ................................................. 160

## Nina May ............................................... 163
*How Should We Then Live?*

## Bradley Mattes, M.B.S. ................................. 177
*Conservatives and Compassion:*
*Equal Partners in Saving Life*

## D. Wilson Nance, Ph.D. ................................. 189
*Larger than Life*
The Conservative Mind Remembers the
  Symbol of Columbia. ..................................... 190
The Conservative Mind Values the
  Conservation of Power .................................... 191
The Conservative Mind Values the Concept of
  Redemption ............................................... 192
The Conservative Mind Values  the Concept of
  Responsibility ........................................... 195
The Conservative Mind Values The Essentiality Of God . 198

## Dean Nelson ................................................. 201
### *What is a Conservative?*
Respect for Tradition .................................................. 201
Pitiful Pitiful Man ...................................................... 203
In the Immortal Words of Frederick Douglass ................ 205
Life is Not Fair.......................................................... 206
Sacred Family ........................................................... 209

## William Owens, Jr. ..................................... 211
### *The DNA of Conservatisim*

## Tony Perkins and Chuck Donovan ................... 213
### *Why the Conservative Mind Matters*

## Dr. Pearl Porter........................................... 221
### *Commitment not Compromise*
The Conservative Mind is Important Because
Freedom is not Free.................................................. 222
The Conservative Mind Matters Because it is not Always
Politically Correct .................................................... 223
The Conservative Mind Matters Because We've Got Some
Folks on "The Hill" Who Just Won't Compromise ......... 225

## Fred Wehba ................................................ 231
### *The Conservative Mind Blessed by God*
### *"Gipper"*

## Epilogue..................................................... 247

# Acknowledgments

Over the course of my work with various organizations, I have made friends and received support, information, and inspiration that have enriched my life and made this publication possible. There are a few people whose contributions are so significant to the project that I want to give them special recognition. I especially want to express my gratitude and love for the most meaningful person in my life, my wife, Deborah Belinda De Sousa Owens, the girl from Panama, who has been my wife for thirteen years and has worked by my side for seventeen years. She has been my most ardent supporter, encourager, critic, and friend. Her ability and willingness to handle her career and professional responsibilities as well as many of my "unusual" responsibilities has enabled me to complete this project.

Second, I would like to thank my diligent and faithful editor, D. Wilson Nance. His availability to discuss thoughts, ideas, and concepts has been extremely helpful. He has a unique ability to see what others don't see. He worked tirelessly and made himself available whenever I called upon him for advice. I am extremely grateful to him for his support and friendship.

He helped to bring this book to fruition. I would also like to thank my son, William Jr., the publisher of this work and my grandson, David who works with his dad. David is only 16 years old and handled this project in a professional manner. I am proud of him. One constant source of inspiration and direction has been my dear friend, Bishop George McKinney who would take my calls on a daily basis at 6:00 AM to discuss this project and other projects we were working on simultaneously. He never tires of taking my calls. I would also like to thank Sharon Jackson of Faith Temple Ministries who helped with whatever I needed when I called upon her. She always has a smile on her face. Most importantly, I wholeheartedly thank all of the contributors who took the time to write a chapter in this book. Your contributions have been monumental, and I am grateful for them.

# Foreword

Based on my 50 plus years of living, studying, growing, learning, working, and reading, I have observed that what most people want in life is to be happy, healthy, reasonably prosperous, and secure. They want to have friends, peace of mind, good family relationships, and most of all they want to have hope.

My wife, Deborah, and I decided to compile a book with a conservative theme because we live by conservative values; we wanted to know how others felt about a conservative mindset. After many hours of pondering and discussing the idea, we decided on a title, *Why the Conservative Mind Matters*. We invited others to contribute a chapter on the topic. This book is the product of 18 individuals, male and female, who took the time to pen their ideas, concepts, and insights as to *Why the Conservative Mind Matters* and why it is important in our daily lives.

**This is not a political book. It does not recognize or advocate any political party or agenda. It is a book that shares the ideas of different individuals of what it means to be a conservative and explains the foundation on which the concept is built.** Of special note are chapters by a fellow minister whom I have only met once. I received a phone call from Chaplain (Major) James

F. Linzey, who is recovering from injuries he received while in training to deploy to Iraq. He is presently at the Walter Reed Army Medical Center in Washington, D.C. He has served in the U.S. Army for twenty-three years. He called to accept our invitation to contribute a chapter to this book. He felt an urgency to be included in this work. His phone call came the day before the book was scheduled to go to print and he asked me if he was too late to send in his chapter. I informed him that the book was behind schedule and we could not delay going to press any longer. He informed me that he had already written two essays that he thought would add to the project. He e-mailed his chapters and I was so moved, I asked him for permission to include both chapters in the book.

I so was inspired by our phone conversations that I felt I should mention him in this foreword. He has a deep desire to serve God and our nation, and I commend him for his years of dedicated service. Be sure you read Major James F. Linzey's two chapters. I am very proud of the work that was submitted by all of our contributing authors. You will find the chapters challenging, informative, scriptural, ethical, motivational, forthright, captivating, and practical. It is a timely and much needed work.

*Bill Owens*
*Memphis, TN*
*October 18, 2008*

# I Am A Conservative Because...

**Bill Owens**

I am a conservative because of the influence of my home and church not because of political or party affiliation.

As a boy, our family lived in two rooms with only an outdoor restroom and water. My mother's sister passed away and her two children came to live with us. My maternal grandmother lived with us also. Consequently, there were three adults, my father, mother, grandmother, and eight children living in these two rooms. Yet, we were happy. In spite of our economic status, my parents spoke of hope and taught us that if we lived a good Christian life, worked hard, studied, and stayed in school that we would one day be able to live the American Dream. The pleasures I longed for were an indoor restroom with a bathtub, a refrigerator instead of an icebox, and a bed of my own. I dreamed, my sisters dreamed, we all dreamed that one day we would get an education, which would enable us to fulfill these dreams.

During this time, blacks suffered many injustices and we were at a disadvantage, but in spite of it all, our parents taught us to love all people regardless of the color of their skin and regardless of how badly they treated us. She would often say:

"God will make the crooked roads straight and turn your nights into days."

She gathered all of us around her; as we sat at her feet, she taught us the Christian values that have sustained us our entire adult lives. My mother only had a sixth grade education, but she was a great orator, wise, and an excellent teacher. Her lessons were simple.

She would say it is not the color of a person's skin that causes him to hate or mistreat another person, but it is what is in his heart. She taught me, sixty years ago, that if blacks had had the same power whites had, blacks would have treated whites the same way. Today, we can look around America and countries in Africa and other nations in the world and see reverse discrimination in action. We did not have luxurious homes, cars, or fine clothes, but we had God, our parents' love and their transforming lessons.

My mother encouraged all of us to get an education, and we did. Today, in spite of the insurmountable odds that faced black men fifty years ago, I am both a minister and an educator. Did I suffer racial prejudice? Yes. But so did millions of other blacks. Nevertheless, we were determined to make something of our lives. We persevered and went to college. Many blacks became doctors, lawyers, nurses, educators, politicians, inventors, philanthropists, musicians, entertainers, journalists, entrepreneurs, and every profession available in this great country.

Therefore, the conservative mind is important because it is built on a firm Scriptural foundation. It is not built on political parties, excuses, handouts, or group conformity.

## I Am a Conservative Because I Care About Scriptural Living, not Merely Scriptural Quotation

For as long as I can remember the great struggle for civil rights has been empowered by the frequent use of the Bible. Its great themes of redemption, patient perseverance, and release from bondage have permeated the rhetoric of the civil rights movement.

But the truth of the matter is that a conservative is much more interested in scriptural living than being able to quote biblical passages into the microphone. Anyone can quote the Bible. And, demagogues who judiciously select words and phrases from Scripture sometimes advance even the most ungodly agenda.

Have you never noticed how abortionists will quote the golden rule of Jesus: "...do unto others what you would have them do unto you"? Then they follow by asking whether you would want to be forced to give birth to and raise a child you didn't want. Then they follow by asking whether you would want to be raised in a family where you weren't loved or even wanted.

They conveniently ignore Jesus' expansion on the golden rule: "...love your neighbor as yourself," as illustrated by the parable of the Good Samaritan. This parable leads us to do what we don't desire, help when it is inconvenient, and give even when it is expensive: and all to someone whom we have every reason not to love.

The unfortunate situation has grown that professing Christians are often more political than Christian. And all the while, they wear Christian robes, quoting Christian scripture, but as Paul said, in their daily living they deny the power thereof.

## I Am a Conservative Because I Care About Family Values Lived, not Merely Family Values Voiced

Closely aligned with my commitment to scriptural living is my commitment to living family values. Family values begin with valuing the family. And what is a family? It begins with one man and one woman and includes their children, biological or adopted.

Of course, some families don't fully meet that definition. This reality has always existed and always will. Yet this reality doesn't weaken the original definition. Every historical variation on the family is derived from the original definition: one man and one woman. It has been this way for five-thousand years.

The courts in two states have a wisdom, which transcends the ages, transcends the sages, and mutates the ministry of every prophet.

Their arrogance is so deep that they celebrate it as wisdom.

They change the definition of family and marriage and then say that the values that support a family ought to apply to their new definition. This is like taking the value that we should support the troops, but then twisting it by saying, we ought to recognize the humanity of all combatants (which we should), then finishing the morph by saying, we ought to honor the terrorists. After all, they are surely misunderstood.

The same-sex marriage agenda is a vampiric perversion that leeches off the genuine creation of God. They contribute nothing, demand everything; and if successful will destroy the very society that has given them life.

## I Am a Conservative Because I Care About Individual Choice, not Merely Public Conformity

As a conservative, I am wholly committed to individual choice, not mere public conformity. I believe I should be free to choose the way I worship God, my friends, my neighborhood, which schools to send my children to, and who to vote for in the election.

The Bible bases our human dignity on the fact that we can and do make choices. Animals don't have the power of choice. Human beings do. Sadly, too many advocates of one position or another wish to create public conformity in all-important matters.

For this aspect of my essay, I want to turn our attention to my concern about choice in public schools.

I strongly support public schools. My wife is a teacher in the public schools, and is in the final year of her doctoral work in one of finest schools for education, Vanderbilt University – a private school. She participates in both private and public education, to the betterment of both. The American dream is not one-size-fits all ideology.

In reality, there is a place in education for both public and private schools. Moreover, the health of our educational system rides on the preservation and support of both systems. We need public schools, schools supported by the community united. However, we also need our charter and private schools.

We are Americans. And the restriction of choice is un-American. Yet, because of poverty, too many Americans are denied this basic American right.

The size of this battle is seen in this bizarre and disheartening fact: the decline of our public schools has mirrored the marginalization of private schools, which are now virtually unavailable to many children. And this has led to another fact, not merely bizarre, but tragic: when I was young, thirty three in one hundred young blacks graduated college. Now, three in one hundred do so. Too many of our young black men end up in prison.

As a conservative, knowing the utter complete determining effect of education on a life, choice is paramount. To deny someone the choice in educational opportunities simply because of their poverty is an abominable violation of basic fair play.

America is not about making people's lives successful. But it is absolutely about making the opportunity for success available equally.

To this end, I support, whole-heartedly and unreservedly, the idea that education tax dollars ought to follow the student, not the school. If a student goes to school A, that is where the taxes for his education should go, if he goes to school B, the same applies.

Without the money following the choice, the choice is aborted completely.

## I Am a Conservative Because I Care About Genuine Diversity, not Merely Group Membership

Conservatives respect individual choice, and individual opinion. And they support strongly the right to disagree significantly. An obvious example of this is my approach to "hate speech."

Hate speech legislation, designed to outlaw certain political and moral ideas, is a politically powerful idea. It has taken strong root in our neighbor to the north, and is on its way to prominence here. But, in fact, hate speech is a misnomer with a heavy political agenda.

While every Christian, if not every human being, understands that hatred of another individual or group is sinful, it is another bizarre twist to assert that strong verbal disagreement amounts to hatred.

The fact is that many people would rather dismiss conservative ideas with venom on the tip of a political knife, than to argue them on their merits. In Canada, my understanding is, that pastors who oppose homosexual behavior as immoral are under a very serious threat of government reprisal. In America, those who oppose homosexual behavior are only slightly less threatened by the broadminded haters of hate speech.

Their own hatefulness strains their credibility as police over speech.

It is easier to shout "Racism!" or "Sexism" or "Eliteism," or any of a dozen "isms" which have become the modern scarlet letter. And then there is the "-phobe" label, that may be more powerful still.

I propose a new one (maybe not so new) that I am sure will never make the network news: conserva-phobe or conservaphobia. We who stiffly uphold conservative family values are all too often exposed to the ridicule of those who mistake human glory for dignity. But I press on, regardless of their derision.

## I Am a Conservative Because I care About Human Dignity, not Merely About Human Glory

The power of these labels, and the hate speech laws that derive from them, is actually neither compassion nor love. It is a selfish desire for glory, which is willing to undermine genuine human dignity.

The pagan Romans built glorious monuments such as the Arch of Titus, which celebrated the inhumane slaughter of their opponents including old men, women, and children. Those who weren't slaughtered were tortured before being allowed to "expire" for the entertainment of passers-by. Crucifixion often lasted days. The rest were sold as slaves and victims of the "circus" where they were humiliated and eviscerated for a crowd gathered to see just such gore. The gore added to the Roman glory.

But at the expense of every human dignity.

They equated the approval of men and women as if that somehow were equal to dignity. But dignity is internal, and often as not is truly described as "a quiet dignity."

I am a conservative, because I care more about genuine dignity than about anyone's opinion of me. And, I care about your dignity than I do about my own opinion of you.

You possess dignity whether I think you do or not. This is an essential error of the abortionist and euthanizer. Even unborn infants have dignity, although they have little human glory. The old and the sick have the divine dignity that God gave them, and this dignity has remained undimmed even in the fading light of human glory.

*I am a conservative.*

## I Am a Conservative Because I was Raised in a God-fearing, Committed Family

I did not get my convictions and values from political parties, the newspaper, or the talking heads on television. I got my convictions from the sweat and tears with which my family raised me. I gained them from the sweat and tears of my own efforts. I gained them from my home through the teachings of my parents and at school by the example set for us by our schoolteachers and leaders. I gained them from a lifetime of exposure to the Scriptures and the guidance of pastors and religious leaders in our community.

I have said throughout this book that I am a conservative but please understand that I don't wear the label of a Republican or Democrat. I am one who fears God and who seeks to follow scriptures not a political party.

I am afraid of no one's opinion. I need no one's approval. The values of scripture truth, genuine family, individual choice, genuine diversity all lead back to their source: the divine dignity of the individual who is committed to loving every other individual, not merely the group into which they may fit.

# The Conservative Movement: A Light in Dark Times

## J. Kenneth Blackwell

As I begin, let me give you some context. I won a football scholarship to Xavier University in Cincinnati, and annually we played the Quantico Marines. In my junior year, a staff sergeant playing across the line from me gave me a physical education that was superior to the academic preparation the Jesuits provided in the classroom. So complete was the whoopin' he put on me that day that I spent almost every day in the intervening year in chapel, praying that he not be sent to Vietnam so I might return the lesson in kind in my senior year.

As my good friends know, God answered my prayers and delivered him unto me. For one complete half, I was returning the lesson. At the beginning of the third quarter, I did one of my patent moves, pushed him to the ground, sidestepped him, and instead of tackling a two hundred forty pound Marine fullback cleanly with my shoulder, my chin got in the way; I was knocked out momentarily.

They sent me to Good Samaritan Hospital, only a stone's throw from where we were playing that Saturday afternoon. They did head X-rays for a concussion, and the results came back negative. They sent me back to the field, where three Jesuits met me at the sideline. They laid hands on me, prayed, and put me back into the game for the balance of the fourth quarter.

Now, we won that game, miraculously, nine to seven. Legend has it that the next day in the Cincinnati Enquirer, the headline blared, for my dear mom to read, "Blackwell: Head X-rays Show Nothing."

But now, all humor aside, I am indeed honored to have been asked to contribute this chapter to this important volume in the company of these influential authors.

## The Fierce Urgency of Now

Our dear brother and master teacher, Russell Kirk, told us that "A culture does not survive and prosper merely by being taken for granted. Active defense is always required."

Some forty four years ago, in a historic city at a historic time in American history, Martin Luther King, Jr. stood at the Lincoln Memorial, and delivered these words: "We have come to this hallowed ground to remind Americans of the fierce urgency of now. This is no time to relax in the luxury of cooling off or to take the tranquilizing drug of gradualism."

I tell you now that I am writing to underscore "the fierce urgency of now." Our revolution of ideas, policy formulations, and citizen action is not over. This revolution requires us to finish the job. It requires us to stand in the gap.

## Moral Coherence and the Promise of America

Some twenty two years ago, I read a book entitled Habits of the Heart, by Robert Bellah and others. In this book they advanced the concept of moral coherence. Moral coherence is when our behavior matches those things we profess to believe. But, when we talk one way, while behaving in another, we create moral incoherence; there is a gap.

Sometimes people call this gap hypocrisy. And while that is true enough, it is a bit to simple. Moral coherence is difficult to achieve, but it is one of the difficult tasks that make the conservative mind all the more important for our willingness to take it on. We are willing to challenge ourselves and then act to live up to the promise of America.

Throughout the last two hundred thirty one years, there have been times in American history when the promise of America has been missed by the practice of her citizens. Whenever we have created this gap between America's promise and our practice, bold men and women are required to stand in the gap, giving their all to close it.

Now, as then, we must act to achieve moral coherence – just like when Americans were debating slavery, the civil rights movement, universal suffrage, the moral outrage of Roe v. Wade, or some of the international tragedies that have beset the human condition.

Now, as then, the challenge is for men and women to close the gap, we who understand that our freedom is inalienable, that we have an intrinsic right to be free.

Our ideas are winning; we have changed the discussions and language in the cloakrooms, the backrooms, and the legislative chambers of our country. But still gaps exist between what we say we believe and what we do in many areas of American life.

So, within our federalist system, it is important that we – in our cities, townships, counties, states all across this country – not only continue to churn out and advance ideas, but actually change the behaviors of men and women who represent us in our government. We must help them close the gap between principle and practice.

Across this entire country, we have more than half a million elected public officials, and what they do – not what they say – matters. It is our job as citizens to hold them accountable so that we complete our revolution. That means we have to rethink our relationships with one another – to advance ideas and change behaviors.

My conservatism comes from practical living experiences. My dad was a meatpacker, and a boxing fanatic. Early in my childhood he enrolled me in a Golden Gloves amateur boxing program. I won my first four bouts with relative ease; the fifth bout, I was hit so hard in the nose I went home and told dad I was going to find a more scholarly career to pursue.

I stayed away from boxing arenas until I was a freshman in college. Father E. J. O'Connor, a senior Jesuit and former Marine, took me and my friend, Benji Schwartz, to the Golden Gloves fights at the old Cincinnati Gardens.

We watched ten bouts. For the eleventh bout, a young boy from the western side of Cincinnati, he too of Irish Catholic heritage, came out. He made the sign of the cross as the bout began. Benji, who was Jewish, elbowed Father and said, "Father, what's the significance of that?" Father said, "Son, it's important, but it ain't enough if he can't fight."

## Advancing the Big Ideas

And I would suggest to you that all of the great research we turn out is not enough – it's important, but it's not enough – if we can't convert it into changed behavior and the advancement of big ideas.

We have done good work. Let's not underestimate the impact that we've had. Many kids today are enjoying an invigorating education because we have been in the forefront, setting the vision, advancing ideas, and motivating citizen action to expand school choice. School choice gives birth to innovation, fosters competition, and improves quality education. It changes the 1965 union model of education that has failed so many of our children. We've been in the forefront of a liberation movement, freeing children who are locked in dysfunctional schools and parents who have been marginalized.

But our job is not done, because the other side has geared up, muscled up, and drawn the fault line – a fault line that divides all America. On one side are those who are the advocates and the apologists for big government; on the other side are those of us who are advocates of freedom and the individual liberties that are so crucial to the American tradition and America's future.

But it doesn't do us any good just to understand that there is a fault line. It really comes back to how we engage our opponents and fight for what we believe. Only this will shape America's future.

In Philadelphia, when the Constitutional Convention was held, then there was a battle of ideas, a test of wills, in hot, uncomfortable rooms. It was at a point of impasse when Benjamin Franklin uttered words that were a harbinger of things to come.

Folks were ready to go their separate ways when he stood up – he was over 80 years old at the time – and said, "Gentlemen, I'm an old man, but this I know: If a sparrow cannot fly without His assistance, then a nation cannot rise without His aid." And at that point, he laid the theoretical understanding on the table that the essence of our free society is that it is built on a moral foundation.

If you listen to the words he spoke, they shape the battle of today. His words gave rise to the second paragraph of our Declaration: "We hold these truths to be self-evident." All of us "are created equal." And we continue to read in that paragraph that we are "endowed by [our] Creator with certain unalienable Rights."

The rejection of these truths is where the fault line originally started, because we believe our human rights are gifts from God, not grants from any government. When you understand that, you never fall into the trap of treating government as God and the provider of our freedoms.

You see, government can do only two things: promote our human liberties and protect them, or abridge and abuse them. It cannot give them to us. When we understand the source of our freedom, it dictates the fight that is in front of us.

And, from this we conservatives begin to understand the importance of our movement. We are a force, by the same providence Franklin and Jefferson spoke of, that will have an impact on American thinking and American behavior.

## Dedication and Purposeful Action

Two hundred and thirty one years ago, only two million people lived under the aegis of democratic government. Today that number is well over two point four billion. So in two hundred thirty one years, we have gone from two million to over two *billion* internationally. America has led the way because we have fought a good fight over the years.

We have understood the power of the human will and have networked human beings as a force focused for change. We know history is not moved by chance; it is moved by men and women of dedication and purposeful action.

When I was growing up in a Cincinnati public housing community, I could get in trouble at one end, and before I got home at the other end, my mom already had the news. That's because I had an "aunt" in every window and on every stoop of that public housing community. The young people today have the Internet. Back then we had the aunty-net; it moved information just as fast.

We are a connected human force augmented by new technologies. If we take advantage of these new technologies, we can move our ideas and change behaviors. But it requires us to stay engaged. Our brilliant history requires us to remain dedicated to those first principles that the modern conservative movement has advocated and advanced.

But the power of the conservative mind is that it understands that in many of our three thousand three hundred counties among fifty states, there are local and regional policy organizations already carrying out the revolution. Our job is to connect them and make them one powerful force.

We must also help our network realize that our work is not finished just because Bill Clinton said, "The era of big government is over." Government gets bigger and our tax code is still the handmaiden of big government, not the engine of economic growth. The model of government schools driven by big unions is still surviving, fattened on plenty of pork. Big government is still real and a threat to our liberty.

The threat is still real because we now have, on the left, apologists for big government who are trying to run God, faith and religion out of the public square. We must understand that this is the ultimate threat to the vibrancy of our freedom movement. They are not merely trying to reestablish the so-called Fairness Doctrine in broadcasting to choke off the voices of the right; they are trying to change the nature and uniqueness of our democracy and culture by running God and faith out of the public square. They have tried to turn us on ourselves. We had best understand that as we work to impact public policy and behavior in the public square.

So our plate is full. We still have work to do. We must be filled anew with the "the fierce urgency of now."

## Punching Holes in the Darkness

Coming up in that working class home, my grandmother was a domestic worker. She used to bring home books given to her by the families for whom she worked. I remember reading a novel about a little boy who spent a lot of time in infirmaries, and one evening – this was in the early 1900s – a nurse came into his room, and she said, "Little boy, what are you doing?"

It was dusk, and he said, "I'm watching the man punch holes in the darkness." She said, "What?" He said, "I'm watching the man punch holes in the darkness."

So she walked over to the window and looked out. What this little boy, who was nine years old or so, saw was a lamplighter going down the street lighting streetlights. In this little boy's mind, this man was punching holes in the darkness.

We have no time to waste cursing the darkness as a conservative movement. It is now our time to light candles with our research and ideas. More importantly, it is time to combine our candles so that we become brighter lights in the darkness of our time: the darkness of big government, the darkness of a faithless culture, the darkness of children being locked out from quality education.

And, we must understand that we've done some good, punched some holes in the darkness. There are eight million people who now have their health savings accounts because we at the state and local levels drove that idea and drove that policy.

We have done some good, but there are still dark clouds. My charge to you is that we recommit ourselves to going out and punching holes in the darkness. Our children and our grandchildren count on us to have that courage.

I close with the words of Winston Churchill. For those of you who, like me, have suffered political setbacks, Mr. Churchill said, "Courage is the ability to go from failure to failure without losing enthusiasm." So I go forth with a smile and a candle to punch holes in the darkness.

J. Kenneth Blackwell is a Senior Fellow for Family Empowerment at the Family Research Council and the Ronald Reagan Distinguished Fellow for Public Policy at the Buckeye Institute for Public Policy Solutions in Ohio. He is a contributing editor of Townhall.com. This chapter is based Mr. Blackwell's remarks delivered at the 30th Annual Meeting of The Heritage Foundation Resource Bank, held in Philadelphia, Pennsylvania, on April 26-27, 2007.

# THE BLACK CHURCH
## Urban America's Voice of Conscience for Family Values

### Tracy Brown

My desire is to share with the world the fact that the Black Church can transform our poorest urban communities by educating and advocating for change by empowering family values. In making this affirmation I am powerfully aware of the problems that the Black inner city communities face. But the conservative family values that have stood the Black community through generations of slavery, oppression, institutionalized segregation and inculturated discrimination, are the very values that will ultimately overcome our current problems.

God has given me the opportunity to participate with both governmental and non-governmental organizations that work to address these problems. So my work and travels have acquainted me with the attempted solutions at close quarters. In working with these groups, I have become ever more confident that the actual solution must involve returning to the conservative conscience of the Black Church in matters of family values.

In this short essay, I need to focus on this question: what are the challenges? I do not have the time here to delve deeply into the methods and policies that will help accomplish this. I will briefly highlight the solutions, then suggest a source where I have expanded on these solutions at length.

The challenge is that within every category of socioeconomic deprivation, Blacks represent six to eight times their proportionate numbers in the general population. The fact is that Blacks are over-represented on this nation's welfare, poverty, unemployment, homeless, drug addiction and crime rolls. This should come as no surprise. After all, it was exactly the goal which Jim Crow laws hoped to achieve. But Jim Crow was not nearly as successful as the welfare policies that began in the 1960's.

Marian Wright Edelman of The Children's Defense Fund, shares these heart breaking statistics:

• 	Every five seconds during the school day, a black public school student is suspended

• 	Every forty six seconds during the school day, a black high school student drops out.

• 	Every minute, a black child is arrested and a black baby is born to an unmarried mother

• 	Every three minutes, a black child is born into poverty.

• 	Every hour, a black baby dies.

- Every four hours, a black child or youth under twenty dies from an accident

- Every five hours, a black youth is a homicide victim

- Every day, a black young person under twenty-five dies from HIV infection and a black youth under twenty commits suicide.

Additionally, consider this astounding and ultimately devastating fact: *Only three out of every one hundred black males entering kindergarten will graduate from college. In the 1950s, under Jim Crow, three out of ten did so.*

But these very policies, empowering certain leaders by entrenching urban black dependency, had a powerful effect on the broader White American culture that it sought to protect. The socioeconomic suppression has infiltrated beyond the Black Community into all races and it has contributed overwhelmingly to the financial problems of our country. Every problem I mentioned (welfare, poverty, unemployment, homelessness, drug addiction and crime) has now become seriously entrenched in the White and Latino urban population as well.

For this reason it is imperative that every American be aware of the problems which have, until recently, been considered Black urban issues. And every American needs to be aware of the powerful solution that the Black Church offers in its advocacy for conservative family values.

Here are a few core values issues that I believe are essential in transforming our nation's poorest communities.

## Parental Guidance

I believe that having no dad affects Black boys' self-esteem. Life with father translates to stronger kids. The lack of fathers contributes to these boys having problems in school, and to participation in gangs as part of their search for male role models.

In the Black Community, there's a slogan: "'Black mothers raise their daughters and love their sons," says Carolyn B. Murray, associate professor at the University of California, Riverside. "It's the father who holds that boy accountable. He has that boy toe the line; he holds the rules and responsibilities."

## Advocacy for "Life"

I believe the African American Church must support life and we must educate our communities to realize how the increase in population provides stability for the future of the African American heritage.

Research shows that today, the average number of children born into a Black marriage is less than 0.9 children per marriage. "The birthrates of black married women have fallen so sharply that absent out-of-wedlock childbearing, the African American population would not only fail to reproduce itself, but would rapidly die off."

The church must understand the significance of the core value of life – that human life begins at conception and unborn babies have the same right to life as all other people.

Blacks make up twelve percent of the population, but have thirty five percent of the abortions in America. Are you aware, that there were fewer Black babies killed during slavery than today? This is true whether you consider it either by the sheer numerical count or by the percentage. We *must* have a conscious and conscientious voice for family values.

## Advocacy for Marriage and Family

The consequences of marriage for African Americans is crucial in the process of community empowerment and economic stability.

"African-Americans are the most un-partnered group in America. Census figures show that thirty five percent of Americans between twenty four and thirty four have never married. For African-Americans, that figure is fifty -our percent."

As abominable as this fact is, it is nonetheless true that during the days of slavery a black child was more likely to grow up living with both parents than he or she is today. Pharaoh (Satan) is still at work.

Due to the high rate of African American single parenting, a black child is more likely to live in poverty and be on welfare. I myself am a child of that population. No one can pretend to me that this fact is other than a reality. It is as real and as devastating to the Black community as a cold gang-banger stiletto in a young boy's back.

The precious value of marriage and of the family is due to the fact that they are willed by God in the very act of creation. At this time in history, the family is the object of numerous forces that seek to destroy or in some way deform it. The well being of society and our own good are intimately tied to the good of the family. As a follower of Jesus we have a Divine command to protect our families from Satan (Pharaoh).

## A National Plan for the Black Church

What is the solution? I believe it is for the Black Church to educate and advocate for family values to change our country. Why the Black Church?

The Black Church community is the only Black institution that has successfully survived slavery, post slavery and our country's economic down times. With such a track record of survival, it is the most qualified institution to empower the urban community. The resilience of its commitment to conservative family values has proven indomitable and effective.

Historically, the Black Church has been a place of worship as well as a social center for the Black community. Now we need the church more than ever. We need to have a unified outlook on how the Black Church can regain our urban communities. Many churches are providing social services to the community.

However, we need to go to the next level by educating the people on core family values issues that would eradicate many of the social and economic concerns in our most depressed communities.

In my most recent book, *Tracy J. Brown, A Moses For Urban America*, I share with the world how the modern day economic system, Pharaoh's system, has contained a generation of people in the mindset of slavery. However, in the book I have also designed a national plan on how "The Black Church," can be the saving grace as the conscience voice of Christ for family values. For *The Black Church's National Plan* visit me on the web at www.urbanawarenessusa.org.

I hope and pray that you are encouraged to press beyond Pharaoh's system and not look back. The journey may be tough at times, but at its conclusion, you will be able to say, "I did not yield to the system. I beat it against all odds! Lack, poverty, even generational poverty has been conquered in my life." What a satisfying proclamation that is!

---

Tracy Brown is President of First Providence Realty, Inc., located in Portsmouth, Virginia, a full service real estate company that specializes in Urban housing for low-to-moderate income families. Brown is the founder of Urban Awareness USA, a recognized non-profit association that assists housing authorities and faith-based organizations to develop community empowerment programs. He is the past local president for National Association of Real Restate Brokers in Portsmouth, VA. Internationally, Brown has assisted with an urban community development project in Benin, West Africa, proposing construction of 1,100 new low-income homes.

Brought up with scarce resources, Brown regularly shares his message on how to rise from adversity to prosperity with audiences of his radio show and motivational sessions. He speaks with the authority of someone who has been down but managed to push himself up. Mr. Brown speaks to Churches throughout the U.S on "Biblical Stewardship: Taking Back the Urban Community and Community Empowerment." In Mr. Brown's other work, he tells of a National Plan for the Black Church to take back The Urban Community. He is the Financial Comptroller of a 1,000-member church in Portsmouth, Virginia and a devoted father and husband.

# Conservative Solutions To Sexual Injustice

## Paul Cameron

Every road children walk and every meal they eat are courtesy of their parents and society. The diversity of things you need, but can't make, is courtesy of other people's children. When people become disabled or grow older, their care is also courtesy of their own or other people's children. This reality underlay the Roman Empire's law that forbade giving inheritances to the childless, Jews demanding leaders have a son, and the Apostle Paul directing younger widows to marry again and have children. Past leaders of our civilization agreed: Citizens should reproduce in order to share in the burden of bearing and raising children to replenish the community and, among other duties care for the aged.

"Surely," it might be said, "with a 401(k) and Social Security the old can pay for assistance." Not quite: For the most part, the old can subsist only if society has produced enough replacement children. Wealth is a promissory note for goods and services. It takes a highly developed, fairly stable society to live up to the promise of "ease for the elderly." As societies run out of children, wealth loses its value (try eating $20 bills). The old can pay for care only if enough children are around to keep the system rolling.

Does this mean the voluntarily childless are ripping off their neighbors? *Absolutely.*

So, why bring up the obvious? Because we are in the midst of a crisis: Western civilization is committing demographic suicide – in part because it has forgotten that citizens have a reproductive duty. Traditionally, sex is supposed to provide society's next generation. But with the exception of the U.S., first-world countries are failing to produce the 2.1 children per woman required for society's continuance. No matter a society's current wealth, the absence of replacement children guarantees a bleak future. Thus, while Europe has an overall birth rate of 1.5 per woman, many countries are at 1.3 or below. So in about thirty-five years, their populations will be halved. For them it is only a matter of a few years until their children will be required to tend the weak and it will be impossible to honor whatever "social security" plan is in place. Given economic interdependence, the demographic collapse of any first-world country will send tremors throughout the West.

The problem of too few children is compounded by the growing proportion of offspring who aren't being raised by married parents. Out of wedlock births assure that ever larger proportions of the West's children will cause problems, especially those associated with delinquency, academic failure and drug addiction.

Having children is transformational. Knowing part of you – the most hopeful and innocent part – is outside your skin, transforms me-centered, selfish, exploratory youth into citizens concerned about what happens outside them – and the future. As parents they become more other-oriented and hence more responsible, knowing their children will eventually depend upon the same stable, prosperous society they have known.

The gay movement exacerbates these problems. Confining one's sexual activity to self-satisfaction steals from those who have made the sacrifice to have children. In addition, homosexuals are, by and large, not be transformed by parenthood. Gays fail to contribute to society's demographic maintenance, disrupt social functioning by spreading disease, and recruit children to their ranks in part because of their self-centeredness. Yet they are being protected by law! Why is this injustice being tolerated?

## Society As a Gigantic Clinic

Tradition held that society must be supported by all able-bodied to provide a stable framework under which the productive could prosper. Three facets of justice were demanded of the able-bodied: economic – everyone should work; criminal – everyone should obey the law; and sexual – everyone should marry and raise children. So Paul decreed those who wouldn't work, shouldn't eat; and those flagrantly unwilling to produce children should be denied sex (the Church punished those engaging homosexual sex severely; the more liberal Thomas Jefferson recommended castration or disfigurement). Today we are currently, proudly replacing a traditional society with a society on its way to becoming a giant mental-and-financial clinic that encourages and protects economic and sexual scofflaws.

Clinics are for victims of accidents, diseases, imprudence or unhappiness. If society is a clinic, then it must use its primary resources (e.g., wealth and honor) to support the troubled, disturbed, poor, or unhappy. Gays have deftly exploited the clinic model. They extol and live a life of sexual irresponsibility – mocking non-homosexuals as "straights" and casting aspersions on married "breeders." Yet gays qualify as "troubled and unhappy" because they feel bad about themselves, test psychologically disturbed, abuse alcohol and drugs, acquire and spread disease, and through their sexual activities generate other physical and social maladies.[1] To "cure" the wounded sensibilities of gays – their feelings of worthlessness and persecution – social esteem is no longer accorded exclusively to those married with children but is extended to "gay partners." Taxes are disproportionately allocated to support gays with AIDS (more than for either heart disease or cancer). And school children are indoctrinated with the joys of homosexuality – without any mention of its abundant sorrows. Under the 'how can society make you feel better about yourself?' model, those whom tradition regards as deadbeats and predators are unjustly in control of the machinery of government and hence the social agenda.

How can the application of conservative principles help reverse these threats to the very survival of our society?

Conservative activists seek to influence society to create responsible adults: citizens who

- Contribute more goods and services than they take

- Obey laws and customs, and

- Get married and raise children

Western civilization is doing exceptionally well at getting citizens to generate more wealth, is passable at maintaining law and order, but failing at getting citizens to get married and raise children. What we need to emphasize should be clear.

Private property and capitalism work best to fulfill our needs for goods and services. Our economic engine has put self-interest into the service of generating bounty. Unfortunately, what works in producing goods and services is *toxic* for the production of well-socialized kids. Among other things, capitalist self-interest cannot be successfully applied to sex. Most economists and political theorists (e.g., Milton Friedman, Murray Rothbard, Adam Smith) wrongly assumed as Konrad Adenauer (German Chancellor, 1957) that "*Kinder haben die Leute immer* – People will always have children.*"* Our civilization has proven otherwise. Today, sex is abundant, but marriage as the prerequisite for sex and children as its fruit is increasingly dismissed as "old fashioned."

The idea that sex is the business of those involved and no one else's has become a bedrock principle of a new kind of injustice – freedom from responsibility, freedom from consequences. Uninhibited sexuality – particularly in today's world where contraception is as available as reproductive duty is absent – is most apt to result in epidemics, abortion, and social decay. Our leaders have forgotten, if they ever consciously realized it, that sex within marriage is to children as private property is to productivity. Either without the other cannot long be sustained as proven in the collapse of the Soviet Union.

So the question is this: What kinds of federal policies might halt the death march of our society and cause it to do an about face? Conservatives are understandably cautious about using government to solve problems, as F.A. Hayek warns against in *The Road to Serfdom*. The result is almost always bureaucratic bungling, some limitation of freedom, and a host of unanticipated consequences. But when the situation is life-threatening – and Europe is literally dying to prove we are in peril – some federal intervention seems warranted – if only to undo the harm already done.

## The Problem of Too Few Children

To a marked degree, the lack of children is the result of economic factors. Put in purely economic terms, we are currently trading babies within marriage for women's contribution to the workforce. In 1800, the average U.S. woman had about seven children, by 1900 it was less than four, and by 2000 it was two. This decline was strongly associated with the proportion of women working outside the home. Career women are less apt to get married, less apt to have children when married, and have fewer children when married. There is little doubt that a significant portion of today's prosperity has been generated by so many women in the workforce. But what does wealth profit a society if it collapses for lack of children? We have to do something which encourages more women to seek fulfillment in rearing children rather than spending their child-bearing years working.

The economic disincentives to marriage are large. Currently, those who get married and have children are punished. Under the current tax code, those married with children pay a considerably higher proportion of their "after expenses" income in taxes than either the unmarried or the married without children. Children, after all, have to eat, be clothed, housed, entertained, and generally nurtured. Parents – who are doing the hard job of having and raising children – typically have much less disposable income than non-parents. By avoiding their reproductive duty, gays have significantly higher disposable income. Is it fair that at the same income level, gays get to play while solid citizens, whose children will help pay the excess costs associated with the gay lifestyle, scrimp?

If women were financially rewarded and socially honored for getting married and raising children, they could enter the labor force after motherhood. If women basically spent the first twenty five or so years of adulthood raising children and then pursued a career, we could have both well-socialized replacement children and part of the boost in the availability of goods and services that working women provide. We would have to give up some growth in wealth, since women can't be expected to work full time and also raise sufficiently well-socialized replacement children.

## Solutions:

*Change the federal tax code* to encourage people to marry and raise children. Grant at least a ten thousand dollar/child exemption (inflation adjusted) from *all* federal taxes/fees for *married couples* raising their own or adopted children. As long as they stay married and live with their children they would be exempt from income, Social Security, and Medicare taxes on that portion of income for each child. This would increase their actual earnings significantly – just when children's extra needs strain the family budget. Single parents would not qualify – we want the well-socialized children that come from married couples. The divorced would only get the exemption for children born within a new marriage.

Ten thousand dollars, in today's dollars, approximates the value of the six hundred dollar exemption per child given in the 1940s and 50s when most mothers did not feel the need to work. The incentive can be increased if we need additional numbers of children. Under this scheme, the average married couple raising three children would pay few federal taxes (about the first thirty five thousand dollars would be tax-exempt) and those raising five would likely pay none – while their kids are under roof. Society would be shifting the bulk of taxation to the single and those married without children (it is only fair that they pay something for their present and future care). When the children left home (or turned eighteen), the couple would pay their full share of taxes (i.e., this is a tax *harbor* not a permanent exemption).

The list of those qualifying for this valuable and honorable benefit should be on-line to reduce fraud and "give credit where great credit is due."

*Give married couples anniversary tax-rewards.* Society profits from stability, and there is evidence that divorce of parents adversely affects even adult children. A two hundred dollar tax exemption per year of continuous marriage would give married couples who "hang in there" some financial reward (those married for forty years would have eight thousand dollars of income exempted from taxation; those married for three years, six hundred dollars). If people remarried, the tax exemption would start ticking anew.

*Change social security and federal pension plans* so that the married who supported their children until they reached adulthood get more income in old age (depending on the number of children). Society should reward the old for service rendered by making the sacrifices to raise quality children – children upon whom all eventually depend.

## Where Persuasion is Insufficient

The Gay Movement is both a cause and a symptom of citizens coming to unjustly believe they have no responsibility to reproduce. As such it must be stopped.

Homosexual sex used to be illegal in every state. Given the current political climate, it appears reasonable to attempt first to remove the *super rights* that gays have acquired over the past few decades. Here are a few steps:

The conferral of *super rights* upon those engaging in homosexuality – since it produces no children, is dangerous to participants and the innocent (e.g., HIV in the blood supply), and often raises social costs (e.g., AIDS)[1] – should be discouraged. States that allow gays to trump the rights of employers and landlords with "gay rights laws" should repeal them. Those who refuse should lose a portion of their benefits under the Stafford Act.

States and municipalities should be encouraged to enact laws with serious penalties for having homosexual sex in public facilities – e.g., rest areas, restrooms, parks, etc. Usually such offenses against the public good are misdemeanors. They should be made felonies. Further, the fines associated with such behavior are minor. Instead, they should be increased substantially.

School children should be taught about the many dangers of homosexual sex. They should be instructed in their reproductive duties and understand the injustice of treating the sexually irresponsible as well as, or even better, than the sexually productive (e.g., the married with children). Any state that refuses should be deprived of federal aid to education. Also, states or municipalities that permit homosexuals as foster or adoptive parents within their jurisdictions should likewise be deprived of federal education funds.

Adoption of these proposals may not reduce the number of citizens with homosexual desires. But they certainly will reduce the number acting upon them. For their sake and as well as that of society, such a reduction would be in everyone's interest.

## In Sum

If enacted, these proposals will encourage more young adults to marry and have children, persuade many tempted by homosexual desires not to act on them, and educate citizens about their reproductive duty. Their enactment will probably reduce abortion and boost adoption by increasing the value of children. Further, because married people are healthier, watch out for and take care of each other, enactment should reduce medical costs. These proposals could head America away from the sexual revolution's notion that sex is a private matter between consenting adults. They should also reinforce America's role as willing to take the steps necessary to continue to be a "shining city on a hill."

### References

1. Cameron, P., Landess, T., Cameron, K. Homosexual Sex as Harmful as Drug Abuse, Prostitution, or Smoking. *Psychological Reports*, 2005; 96:915-963.

2. Cameron, P., Cameron, K. What Proportion of Newspaper Stories about Child Molestation Involves Homosexuality? *Psychological Reports*, 1998; 82:863-871; Cameron, P. Molestations by Homosexual Foster Parents: Newspaper Accounts vs. Official Records. *Psychological Reports* 2003; 93:793-802.

Cameron P., Cameron, K. Did the APA Misrepresent the Scientific Literature to Courts in Support of Homosexual Custody? *Journal of Psychology*, 1997;131:313-332; Cameron, P., Landess, T., Cameron, K. Errors by the American Psychiatric Association, the American Psychological Association, and the National Educational Association in Representing Homosexuality in *Amicus* Briefs about Amendment 2 to the U.S. Supreme Court. *Psychological Reports*, 1996; 79:383-404.

© 2008, Paul Cameron

Paul Cameron received the Ph.D. in 1966 from the University of Colorado in psychology (social personality). He has taught at the university level for 14 years (including Fuller Graduate School of Psychology and the University of Nebraska), then joined Family Research Institute as Chairman in 1982.

He was the first scientist (in 1967) to document the health effects of secondhand tobacco smoke upon resident children and spouses. He then explored the social-psychology of secondhand tobacco smoke and 'quarantining' of smokers (1968-72). His interests started to focus on AIDS and the gay movement, and he had a significant hand in getting gay blood barred from the blood banks in 1985. Along the way he demonstrated the shortened lifespan of both men and women who engage in homosexuality.

Of late he's been concerned about the movement to let homosexuals raise other people's children as either foster- or adoptive-parents. He's shown that the American Psychological Association and the National Association of Social Workers have misrepresented the scientific literature on how well homosexuals do as parents to courts and the scientific community. Additionally, he has gotten the investigations of sexual abuse from the state of Illinois on kids being fostered or adopted. It turns out that about a third (34%) of those molestations are homosexual (2003). Similarly, in just about every English-speaking country, a third or more of molestations of pupils by teachers is homosexual. By examining court records he and his colleagues have found that homosexual parents are considerably more apt to abuse their children—physically, sexually, or emotionally.

He has published over 40 scientific articles about homosexuality, am the American editor of the Empirical Journal of Same-Sex Sexual Behavior, and have served as a reviewer for the American Psychologist (1978), Gerontologist, J of Gerontology, British Medical J (2004), Canadian Medical Association J (2005), Postgraduate Medical J (2006-7), and Psychological Reports (2008).

He is licensed in Nebraska (No. 10034; inactive status), and has been employed as expert by the city of Houston, the states of TX, LA, MT, UT, & CO; and the federal governments of Canada (1990, 2004) and US. (1993). He has given expert testimony regarding homosexual custody in 11 states: MI, OH, WA, CO, TX, NY, VA, FL, GA, NC, & MO.

He is listed in a number of Who's Who (World, Science and Engineering, US, East, Midwest, West, Innovators in Science).

He was born November 9, 1939 (but can't remember it), has been married since 1969 to Ginny (and remembers that); they have 3 children and 11 grandchildren (all of whom are memorable).

# Why I am a Conservative

## Charles Colson

A few years after I was released from prison, my old friend, the estimable William F. Buckley, invited me to be a guest on his award-winning PBS program "Firing Line." When he asked about prisons, I told Buckley they were a complete failure, that human nature cannot be reformed by putting people in warehouses. Fresh in my mind were the men I'd seen in prison who had been unjustly sentenced or were victims of racial disparity in sentencing. I saw how futile it was to cast them back out on the streets with $50, a bus ticket home, an old suit of clothes, and a guard at the gate saying "See you in three weeks."

Near the end of the interview I made an impassioned plea for justice and a more effective way for people to be punished when they break the laws of society. Morton Kondracke, the moderator of the program who at that time considered himself a liberal, was clearly astonished with my answer. "Mr. Colson," he said, "I thought you were a conservative. What are you doing advocating prison reform?"

It was all I could do to hold back laughter. Sure, I know the popular perception of conservatives: plump, white men in three-piece suits, smoking cigars in the plush leather chairs of their males-only club, advocating low taxes, smaller government, and big business. That's the stereotype. Kondracke, of course, was merely parroting the ideological perceptions that are associated today with people we call liberals and people we call conservatives. Sadly, all these years later, that same confusion dominates public debates in America and all of our seemingly endless election campaigns.

We need to first understand that the true conservative is never beholden to any ideology. Ideologies, after all, are the man-made formulations and doctrines that both the right and the left in modern American politics adopt, like the agendas of political parties. But true conservatives are not guided by any man-made formulations; they're guided by revealed truth.

Russell Kirk, the great Catholic scholar whose writings have so influenced me, says that ideology consists of "the abstract designs of coffee-house philosophers." Most tend to be utopian and end up serving not the welfare of the people, but the interests of power-seekers. The best evidence for this wisdom is found in the wreckage left in the 20th century by all the hideously misguided "isms" of communism and national socialism, of scientism or humanism—all of which promised to lead us to a worldwide utopia. They led instead to the gulags, the Holocaust, and the killing fields of Cambodia. The ideologue's utopian promise is just a means to power which ends up invariably in tyranny for the masses.

Conservatism, on the other hand, is not a set of doctrines, according to Kirk, but "a state of mind, a type of character, a way of looking at the civil social order." They are, Kirk says, the inner order of the soul, and the outer order of the common-wealth.

The conservative draws his wisdom and guidance from the truth that has been revealed to him by those who have gone before us. For Christian believers, of course, that is found in scripture. But all true conservatives look to natural law, that body of moral truth which all people have believed at all times in all places. "Moral truths," Kirk argued, "are permanent." There is an existing moral order which is accessible to all. And so the conservative is one who defends the moral order. To be a conservative is to belong to what the great English poet T. S. Eliot described as the society of "permanent things."

So defending the moral order is the first task of the conser-vative; and the first truth of the moral order is that human life has innate dignity. All Christians believe this, as do classical conservatives. Jefferson, who was not a Christian, penned these unforgettable words in the Declaration of Independence, "We hold these truths to be self-evident, that all men are created equal, that they are endowed by their Creator with certain un-alienable rights, that among these are Life, Liberty, and the pur-suit of Happiness." (By "happiness" Jefferson meant the classi-cal definition: the pursuit of virtue.) Those memorable words rang in my ears when I signed up to be an infantry officer in the Marine Corps during the Korean War. I'd give my life to de-fend those self-evident truths.

So why then should it surprise commentators that we conservatives care about prisoners and justice and the poor? If the moral order is self-evident, that **all** humans are created equal and endowed by their Creator with certain unalienable rights, Christians and true conservatives are bound to defend these truths. Which is why human rights campaigns have been so often been led by them.

William Wilberforce is a prime example. He was, remember, not only a courageous Christian leader of Britain's abolitionist movement; he was also a conservative political leader in Parliament. When in 1787 he made the decision to challenge the slave trade—then the biggest source of revenue to the British Empire—he was warned that he, an aristocrat, would lose his social status and his political base by fighting against the power structures of England; that he might never be Prime Minister. But this didn't deter him in the slightest. True conservatives, as we will see, are interested in principle, not power. So Wilberforce undertook what became a 20-year campaign against the vested slaving interests in the Parliament.

Think of it: The British government, as late as the early 19th century, sanctioned the slave trade; African bodies stuffed in the holds of ships, thrown overboard when they got sick, and the survivors deposited in the West Indies. No wonder conservatives are at times distrustful of big government and entrenched power interests. But against all odds, Wilberforce beat the system. He was a conservative who did radical things. In 1807 the slave trade was abolished by the Parliament, and just a few days before Wilberforce died in 1833, slavery itself was abolished in the British Empire.

After his death, Wilberforce's followers carried on his many, many campaigns to reform the prisons, free children from slave labor in British factories, promote safety in the coal mines, end dueling, and a hundred other worthy causes. In fact, a great Christian revival swept through England, lasting a century and culminating with William Booth's "Salvation Army" moving into the slums of East London to help the poor and the homeless.

Conservatives continued not only to reform England in the 19th century, but America, as well. Lincoln, after all, was a political conservative, without whose courage and willingness to follow principle, even at his own political expense, slavery might not have been ended here.

Conservatives today do the same kinds of thing—to the consternation of the press, which has totally mischaracterized us—especially conservative who are Christians. In the early days of the Bush presidency, Bill Bennett and I visited Karl Rove and later, the President. Our first appeal was to bring an end to slavery in Sudan and persecution of Christians in southern Sudan. Bush immediately picked up the cause and appointed a special emissary. Peace was soon achieved in the south, the slave trade ended. We then turned to the issue of sexual trafficking, which the prior administration had refused to deal with. (Bill and Hillary Clinton had the idea that sexual trafficking "empowered" women by giving them jobs in the prostitution industry.) When I told Bush about this face to face, he was horrified.

Our next goal was to encourage President Bush's campaign to eradicate AIDS in Africa. Bush more than tripled the amount of money spent by prior administrations, and declared it to be the national purpose to achieve an end to the AIDS epidemic. He worked closely with many of us in the Christian community for the application of faith-based principles in African nations—abstinence first, monogamy second, and condoms only if necessary.

When the President addressed the United Nations on sexual trafficking, liberals in the press were bewildered. Why would a right-winger do such things? And then word leaked out that Franklin Graham and I and some others had been consulted in the President's foreign policy initiatives. Elizabeth Bumiller, then the White House correspondent for the *New York Times*, visited my office. "I don't understand," she said, "why evangelicals are concerned with these things. I thought your issues were abortion and the family." I tried to give Ms. Bumiller some lessons in what Christians and classical conservatives believe. And the resulting front-page story in the *New York Times* had a man-bites-dog character.

Secular elites simply don't get it. They are so enmeshed in ideology themselves that they assume everybody on the other side, politically, is captive to a contrary ideology.

But the conservative is never in pursuit of ideology, nor does the true conservative seek power for his own sake. The reason principle is more important than power is that true conservatives have a modest view of what government can do. And rather than promoting unrestricted government power, conservatives work for a balance of powers, where limits are placed on how much government can interfere with the intermediate institutions like churches and neighborhood groups, the ones that get the real work of building civic responsibility done—what the conservative English statesman and founder of the modern conservative movement, Edmund Burke, called "the little platoons of society."

This is why conservatives have been in the vanguard of promoting judges who interpret the law, not make it. To give unrestricted power to unelected judges is to deny the established moral law and the whole conservative concept of limited power and the consent of the governed.

We just don't trust unlimited power in anyone's hands because a conservative has a realistic view of human nature. We know, as the Bible teaches and human experience dictates, that human beings are fallen, that we are prone to be corrupted by power.

I've experienced this in my own life, when I went to the White House. It would be hard to find a more self-righteous man than the then 37-year-old Charles Colson, former lieutenant in the Marines, proud of his country, a successful lawyer who was taught at his father's knee to never tell a lie. That was the great cardinal sin in my Dad's eyes. In fact, I had a puritanical upbringing: right and wrong and honesty were drilled into my head. When President Nixon asked me to be his Special Counsel, it meant surrendering a very lucrative law practice. But I did it. Just as in the days when I was a Marine, I heard those words from the Declaration of Independence and felt gratitude to my country. So when I arrived at the White House, the first thing I did was put everything I had earned into a blind trust in a bank in Boston. I also vowed that I would not see any of the clients I had dealt with when I was practicing law. No one, I thought, could ever corrupt Chuck Colson.

But self-righteousness is a deadly thing. I was blinded to the subtle temptations of power. I didn't even realize that it was happening to me, and I ended up in prison.

There are days when I want to shout from the rooftops: all human beings are corruptible. Lord Acton was right, power does corrupt, and absolute power absolutely corrupts. And all of us, left to our baser instincts, will end up doing the wrong thing.

From this conviction flow two great concerns. The conservative believes that personal character and integrity are more important even than competence when someone is to be entrusted with power. Integrity means wholeness, that what a person does in private will reflect what he does in public; what a person does when no one is looking is what defines who he is. Honor, duty, trust—these are the things that really matter. True conservatives—and I know many who have failed at this—put principle and integrity above power. A true conservative does not seek office to gain power, but rather to have the opportunity to preserve the moral order and defend the truth with which he is entrusted.

The second conviction that flows from this, of course, is that government isn't the be-all and end-all. Big government isn't necessarily a bad thing if it operates efficiently to keep order and produce the maximum justice for human beings. But our founders understood there had to be a balance between government maintaining order (by force) and guaranteeing liberty for citizens. Order is the first biblical duty of government, liberty the first fruit of the moral order. The founders thus called this nation an experiment in "ordered liberty."

Like Burke, we believe a society should encourage civic duty, citizens acting responsibly and governing themselves. Government must respect what in the Reformation was called sphere sovereignty; government not dominating all of society by acting like the traffic cop, but encouraging all the competing groups of society—family, church, civic institutions, education and the like—to do what they do best.

One of the prime conservative virtues, which goes back to the Greeks, is prudence. That is, understanding the limits of humans, and the need for restraining political power, but working to make policies which are efficacious, that is, those which will produce the most lasting benefits. Therefore, we examine things as to whether they produce a long-term good for people as opposed to a momentary political solution.

I saw how this worked out when I was called by God to spend my life serving in the prisons. For a century we had the utopian idea that prisons could "cure" crime. In prison I had seen the futility of the current system, as I told Bill Buckley. Our prisons were not institutions for rehabilitation; they were graduate schools for crime. I'd see inmates sitting around at night talking with each other, actually teaching one another how to commit their next crime without getting caught. When prisoners are released, they are totally ill-prepared for society. Two-thirds come back within three years.

When I began the ministry of Prison Fellowship, it was right at the beginning of the great surge in prison construction. When I was released in 1975 there were 229,000 Americans incarcerated; today there are 1.5 million in prisons and another 700,000 in jails.

So I began to ask why we were building so many prisons. I studied what were then the prevailing sociological theories about crime. Led by a sociologist at Indiana University in the 20s, the dominant view was that crime was caused by deprivation, poverty, racism, environment, etc. The liberal theory went that if we built these correctional institutions, these poor offenders, who were victims of society, could be "resocialized" (yes, that was the operative word in the 30s and 40s when dormitories were being built, and was the operative thesis in the 60s.) Ramsey

Clark, who was Lyndon Johnson's Attorney General, said "Poverty is the cause of crime." Hubert Humphrey agreed, saying that if he had to live in a slum, he'd try to burn it down.

This was the worst signal imaginable to send to millions of inner city residents who began to see themselves as victims. They weren't responsible for their behavior, so rebelling wasn't a bad idea after all. Hence the tremendous surge in crime. Do you see the pattern here? The liberal ideologue believes that we can create an institution and find the utopian solution to crime. The prison, which in the Bible was restricted for debtors, is a classic example.

But the conservatives of that era, or so they were called— the law-and-order crowd, of which I had once been a part, were no better. They believed that human beings were rational calculators, and if you increased the penalties they would commit fewer crimes—a big utopian idea; reform them to rationally decide not to commit crimes. But people are never scared out of committing crimes. The deterrent theory has proven generally ineffective.

So today's "liberal" ideologues and "conservative" ideologues were responsible for building a prison nation in America which today incarcerates 1 out of every 100 Americans and 1 out of every 15 black adults. Such are the consequences of misguided utopianism.

But two Jewish psychiatrists in the 70s made an astounding discovery. Doctors Samenow and Yochelson, predisposed to believe that crime was caused by poverty and racism, did a 17-year longitudinal study and found, to their great surprise, that the cause of crime was, as they put it, "wrong moral decisions." The offender was responsible for his own behavior? It was a shocking conclusion. But it was confirmed a decade later by Professors Wilson and Hernnstein at Harvard, who did a second study and also found that crime was caused by the lack of moral training during the morally formative years.

For me it was an "aha!" moment. Modern liberalism says that people are good in their natural state (Rousseau's argument), corrupted only by our institutions. So if things go wrong, we fix the institutions. Conservatives on the other hand, have been right all along that human beings by nature are fallen, and we are therefore responsible for our own behavior. The way we fix problems is not to blame society but to reform ourselves. We're not victims. There is no utopian big government answer. Respecting and relying on religious teaching, Kirk said, is a cardinal tenet of conservatism.

This is what turned me into a prison reformer. Believing in the existing moral order and the dignity of human beings, I have been fighting ever since against an oppressive system that is government utopianism run amuck. Let's find community solutions; prudent approaches with alternatives to incarceration. Let's work to restore the broken families in American life, which is the real cause of crime. We're never going to defeat crime or reform prisons until we recognize that the problem is a moral one, not a social or economic one.

Above all, conservatives understand the limits of our own ability. We start with very modest expectations about our own capacities, and a reliance on the wisdom of those who preceded us; (a bracing dose of modest expectations would do a lot to cure the current political craze in America). Kirk put it well: relying on what's been revealed to us, conservatives "sense that modern people are dwarfs on the shoulders of giants, able to see further than their ancestors only because of the great stature of those who have preceded us in time." I came face to face with this truth when I visited Mars Hill in Athens, where the Apostle Paul confronted the Areopagus, the council of elders, (Acts 17). The famed Mars Hill is simply a huge boulder which sits on the side of a hill, at the top of which is the great landmark of Athens, the Parthenon. Ascending this slippery rock is no small feat. Little footholds are carved in the side, and only a lover of history would dare go up and down.

When I got to the top, I could see all of Athens spread before my eyes, and could only imagine what it must have been like for Paul, a Jew, to come into this center of culture and learning, a city which prided itself on producing the great philosophical wisdom of the ages. To stand before the power structure of the day and to give that amazing message which drew upon the poetry of the Greeks, their temple to an unknown god—was incredible. And then he told them what they had never known—that Jesus Christ had been bodily raised from the dead, and in Him was The Truth that we could know. He died for our sins, and He reigns today.

Imagine what the wise men of Athens thought, looking at him. The scripture tells us that he convinced only a very few that day. I wonder if he was discouraged. He must have felt terribly lonely. But as I stood on that spot, shivers running up and down my spine, I looked over to the Parthenon, the great ancient structure in partial ruins, and I remembered that for centuries on Good Friday, the flag has been lowered to half-staff and raised full on Easter Sunday morning as Christians around the world celebrate the Resurrection. In that very spot where only a few followed Paul that day, was delivered a message, the truth of which has transformed hundreds of millions in the 2,000 years since. That transformation continues today. It is the faith entrusted to the saints once for all, and it endures.

Revering what is true as opposed to embracing utopian fads of the day is what marks the conservative disposition. The way all true Christians and classical conservatives see the world has little to do with ideology.

But all the debates we're watching in American life today are debates of ideology: ideology of the right, which wants perhaps lower taxes and less government, and a stronger military versus the ideology of the left, which is liberalism run amuck: the idea that each individual must be allowed to determine for himself the meaning of life, shuck off all restraints, and mock the moral order. We need to understand that today's political battles are being fought over ideological formulations arising from the political platforms of the two differing political parties.

But we should not be taken in. We may pursue the things the world calls liberal, like prison reform and help for the poor, because doing so is in the pursuit of human dignity. And we might reject those things ideology labels as conservative, like favoring big business, or being anti-government. Faithful Christians and classical conservatives, regardless of the political party we support, must rely on revealed truth to discern what is wise and prudent in public life. The great line of demarcation in modern politics, as Kirk calls it, is, to paraphrase Eric Voegelin, the great 20th century political theorist, not a division between liberals on one side as they are currently known, and totalitarians on the other, as the right is labeled. Rather, there are, on one side of that line, men and women who believe that the temporal order is the only order, that material needs can explain all of life, and so they may do what they like while in power, providing they can meet those needs. But on the other side are conservatives, those who recognize an enduring moral order, fallen human nature, and who have a high regard for the spiritual as well as the temporal order.

The great virtue of prudence, which the conservative clings to, is the antidote to the ideological horrors of the 20th century that now lie on the ash heap of history. True conservatism marks a way of bringing human progress to its fullest flourishing.

More than 30 years ago, Charles W. Colson was not thinking about reaching out to prison inmates or reforming the U.S. penal
system. In fact, this aide to president Richard Nixon was "incapable
of humanitarian thought," according to the media of the mid-1970s.
Colson was known as the White House "hatchet man," a man feared
by even the most powerful politicos during his four years of service to
President Nixon. When news of Colson's conversion to Christianity
leaked to the press in 1973, the Boston Globe reported, "If Mr. Colson
can repent of his sins, there just has to be hope for everybody." Colson
would agree.

In 1976, Colson founded Prison Fellowship Ministries,
which, in collaboration with churches of all confessions and denomi-
nations, has become the world's largest outreach to prisoners, ex-pris-
oners, crime victims, and their families. Colson has spent the last 25
years as head of Prison Fellowship Ministries.

Because Colson understood that the work of changing prisoners' lives should be a global endeavor, Prison Fellowship International was formed in 1979 under his direction. It has since expanded
to include national chapters in 88 countries.

In recognition of his work, Colson received the prestigious
Templeton Prize for Progress in Religion in 1993, donating the $1
million prize to Prison Fellowship. Colson's other awards have included the Humanitarian Award, Dominos Pizza Corporation (1991);
The Others Award, The Salvation Army (1990); several honorary
doctorates from various colleges and universities (1982–2000); and
the Outstanding Young Man of Boston, Chamber of Commerce
(1960).

Despite his work critiquing the culture, Colson's heart is ever
with the prisoner. He has clearly never forgotten the promise he made
to his fellow inmates during his brief stay in prison: that he would
"never forget those behind bars."

# Conserving the
# Freedom of Religion

## William J. Federer

At different times, "conservative" has had different meanings.

In a 1973 interview, then Governor Ronald Reagan stated:

The classical Liberal, during the Revolutionary time, was a man who wanted less power for the king and more power for the people. He wanted people to have more say in the running of their lives and he wanted protection for the God-given rights of the people. He did not believe those rights were dispensations granted by the king to the people, he believed that he was born with them. Well, that today is the Conservative.

Conservative comes from conserve, derived from the Latin *comservare*, meaning "to preserve, to protect, keep or guard."

A leader who wanted to preserve the God-given rights of individuals from big government was Thomas Jefferson. Jefferson drafted the Declaration of Independence, served as Governor of Virginia and as the third U.S. President. He approved the Louisiana Purchase and commissioned Lewis and Clark to explore it. He sent Marines to fight Muslim Barbary Pirates of Tripoli and founded the University of Virginia.

But Jefferson is also known for his phrase "a wall of separation between church and state."

After the 1947 Everson vs. Board of Education case, big government has used Jefferson's phrase to limit religious freedom, but examining Jefferson's background gives a different perspective.

Jefferson was baptized, married and buried in the Church of England, or Anglican Church, as recorded in his family Bible.

He lived in Virginia, which had an "establishment" of the Anglican Church from 1606 to 1786. Establishment meant mandatory membership, mandatory taxes to support it, and one could not hold public office unless a member.

Over time, "dissenting" religious groups entered colonial Virginia.

In the 1620's, persecuted Presbyterians and Puritans began arriving from Ireland and England, followed by Quakers in the 1650's.

Persecuted Huguenots began arriving from France in the 1670s, followed by Lutherans, Mennonites and Moravian Brethren arriving from Central Europe in the 1680's.

In the 1750s, a movement within the Anglican Church, called Methodism, spread to America. In the decades prior to the Revolution, Baptists became the target of severe persecution in Virginia.

Francis L. Hawks wrote in Ecclesiastical History, 1836:

"No dissenters in Virginia experienced for a time harsher treatment than the Baptists. They were beaten and imprisoned, and cruelty taxed ingenuity to devise new modes of punishment and annoyance."

Following George Whitefield's Great Awakening revival, Jefferson's Albemarle County saw Baptist, Presbyterian and Methodist revivals. Even Jefferson's daughter, Mary, later attended a Baptist revival preached by Lorenzo Dow.

Dolly Madison, wife of James Madison, reported that in 1774 Jefferson dined with Baptist Pastor Andrew Tribble at Monticello, where Jefferson commented that Baptist church government "was the only form of pure democracy that exists in the world. ...It would be the best plan of government for the American colonies."

During the Revolution, Anglican ministers sided with King George, who was head of the established Anglican Church. This resulted in patriotic parishioners migrating away from the established church into "dissenting" churches.

In 1777, Jefferson started a dissenting church, the Calvinistical Reformed Church, meeting in the Albemarle County Courthouse. Drawing up its bylaws, Jefferson's novel idea was for this to be a "voluntary" church, supported only by attendees.

Jefferson's memorandum book shows he contributed to their evangelical pastor, the Rev. Charles Clay, as well as to missionaries and other churches:

I have subscribed to the building of an Episcopal church, two hundred dollars, a Presbyterian, sixty dollars, and a Baptist, twenty-five dollars.

After the Revolution, Virginia rewrote its laws removing references to the King. Dissenting churches lobbied Jefferson to "disestablish" the Anglican Church.

Jefferson responded by writing his Bill for Establishing Religious Freedom. In 1779, a fellow member of Jefferson's Calvinistical Reformed Church, Col. John Harvie, introduced the bill in Virginia's Assembly.

After three of Jefferson's children died, then his wife in 1782, Jefferson suffered severe depression, burned all of his wife's letters and withdrew from politics. Trying to help, Congress asked Jefferson in 1784 to go France, which was going through its period of "French infidelity" prior to the bloody French Revolution. After this, Jefferson tended more toward a Deist-Christian, though in later life he was described as a "liberal Anglican."

Jefferson's bill, which he noted on his gravestone, passed Virginia's Assembly, January 16, 1786:

"Almighty God hath created the mind free....All attempts to influence it by temporal punishments...are a departure from the plan of the Holy Author of religion, who being Lord both of body and mind, yet chose not to propagate it by coercions on either, as was in His Almighty power to do....Be it enacted...that no man shall...suffer on account of his religious opinions."

Virginia's disestablishment of the Anglican Church in 1786 would never have passed had not Methodist Bishop Francis Asbury split the popular Methodist movement away from the Anglican Church in 1785.

The effort against disestablishing, led by notables like Patrick Henry, was later labeled "antidisestablishmentarianism."

Virginia soon built its first Jewish synagogue in 1789 and first Catholic church in 1795.

Jefferson was friends with Virginia Baptist Preacher, John Leland, even hearing him preach at a church service on "separation of church and state" in the U.S. Capitol.

Leland, who was considering running for Congress, wanted an Amendment to the Constitution protecting religious liberty, so he reportedly met with James Madison near Orange, Virginia. Upon Madison's promise to introduce what became the First Amendment, Leland had Baptists support him.

Leland then went to help Baptists in Connecticut where there was an establishment of the Congregational denomination from 1639 until 1818.

In his *Rights of Conscience Inalienable*, 1791, Leland demanded not just toleration, but equality:

"Every man must give account of himself to God, and therefore every man ought to be at liberty to serve God in a way that he can best reconcile to his conscience. If government can answer for individuals at the day of judgment, let men be controlled by it in religious matters; otherwise, let men be free."

Connecticut Baptists, of the town of Danbury, then petitioned President Jefferson, October 7, 1801:

"Sir...Religion is at all times and places a Matter between God and Individuals – That no man ought to suffer in Name, person or effects on account of his religious Opinions....But Sir...what religious privileges we enjoy...we enjoy as favors granted, and not as inalienable rights."

Danbury Baptists continued:

"Sir, we are sensible that the President of the united (sic) States is not the national Legislator and...cannot destroy the Laws of each State; but our hopes are strong that the sentiments of our beloved President...like the radiant beams of the Sun, will shine & prevail through all these States...May the Lord preserve you safe from every evil and bring you at last to his Heavenly Kingdom through Jesus Christ our Glorious Mediator."

On January 1, 1802, Jefferson wrote his famous letter agreeing with Danbury's Baptists:

"Gentlemen...Believing with you that religion is a matter which lies solely between man and his God, that he owes account to none other for faith or his worship, that the legislative powers of government reach actions only, and not opinions, I contemplate with solemn reverence that act of the whole American people which declared that their legislature should "make no law respecting an establishment of religion, or prohibiting the free exercise thereof," thus building a wall of separation between Church and State."

Jefferson continued:

"Adhering to this expression of the supreme will of the nation in behalf of the rights of conscience, I shall see with sincere satisfaction the progress of those sentiments which tend to restore man to all his natural rights, convinced he has no natural right in opposition to his social duties. I reciprocate your kind prayers for the protection and blessing of the common Father and Creator of man."

Baptists were familiar with Jefferson's metaphor "wall of separation," as Baptist founder of Rhode Island, Roger Williams, used it in his *Bloody Tenet of Persecution for Conscience Sake*, 1644:

"Jews under the Old Testament...and...Christians under the New Testament...were both separate from the world; and that when they have opened a gap in the hedge, or wall of separation, between the garden of the Church and the wilderness of the world, God hath ever broken down the wall itself...And that therefore if He will ever please to restore His garden and paradise again, it must of necessity be walled in peculiarly unto Himself from the world."

Jefferson viewed the "wall" as limiting the federal government from "intermeddling" in church government, as explained in his letter to Samuel Miller, January 23, 1808:

"I consider the government of the United States as interdicted [prohibited] by the Constitution from intermeddling with religious institutions, their doctrines, discipline, or exercises. This results not only from the provision that no law shall be made respecting the establishment or free exercise of religion, but from that also which reserves to the states the powers not delegated to the United States [10th Amendment]."

Jefferson continued:

"Certainly no power to prescribe any religious exercise, or to assume authority in religious discipline, has been delegated to the General [Federal] government....Every religious society has a right to determine for itself the times for these exercises, and the objects proper for them, according to their own particular tenets."

"The federal government was not limited, though, from spreading religion in Western territories, as on April 26, 1802, Jefferson extended a 1787 act of Congress where lands were designated:

For the sole use of Christian Indians and the Moravian Brethren missionaries for civilizing the Indians and promoting Christianity..."

And again, December 3, 1803, Congress ratified Jefferson's treaty with Kaskaskia Indians:

"Whereas the greater part of the said tribe have been baptized and received into the Catholic Church...the United States will give annually, for seven years, one hundred dollars toward the support of a priest of that religion, who will engage to perform for said tribe the duties of his office, and also to instruct as many of their children as possible....And the United States will further give the sum of three hundred dollars, to assist the said tribe in the erection of a church."

Twelve years before his death, Jefferson shared his personal views to Miles King, September 26, 1814:

"We have heard it said that there is not a Quaker or a Baptist, a Presbyterian or an Episcopalian, a Catholic or a Protestant in heaven; that on entering that gate, we leave those badges of schism behind....Let us be happy in the hope that by these different paths we shall all meet in the end. And that you and I may meet and embrace, is my earnest prayer."

When John Adams' wife died, Jefferson wrote to him, November. 13, 1818:

"The term is not very distant, at which we are to deposit...our sorrows and suffering bodies, and to ascend in essence to an ecstatic meeting with the friends we have loved and lost, and whom we shall still love and never lose again. God bless you and support you under your heavy affliction."

Originally, the first ten amendments were viewed as limitations or handcuffs which the States insisted be put on the new Federal Government's power to keep it from becoming a big centralized monster like King George III. The newly independent States wanted to make sure the new Federal Government was tied up with chains so that when it took life it would not become an out-of-control Frankenstein.

But after the Fourteenth Amendment was passed in 1868 to guarantee rights to freed slaves, activist judges began viewing the Fourteenth Amendment as an exciting box of chocolates with which they could re-interpret eight of the first ten amendments.

Interestingly enough, they could not re-interpret the Ninth and Tenth Amendments, as they referred to: "powers not delegated to the United States by the Constitution...are reserved to the States respectively, or to the people."

U.S. Supreme Court Justice Joseph Story, who founded Harvard Law School, wrote in his *Commentaries on the Constitution*, 1833:

The whole power over the subject of religion is left exclusively to the State governments, to be acted upon according to their own sense of justice and the State Constitutions.

*John Bouvier's Law Dictionary*, published in Philadelphia by the J.B. Lippincott Company, 1889, stated in its definition of "Religion":

"The Christian religion is, of course, recognized by the government, yet...the preservation of religious liberty is left to the States."

In other words, the reason the Federal Constitution says little about religion was not because the founders thought religion unimportant. To the contrary, they thought religion was so very important, they wanted to keep it under States' jurisdiction, similar to local control of the school board, local control of the fire department and local control of the police department.

Like a race track with 13 lanes, jurisdiction over religion was left to the States, and different States broadened religious freedom at different speeds - Rhode Island and Pennsylvania being way out in front and Connecticut and Massachusetts lagging behind.

But after the Fourteenth Amendment was passed in 1868, Federal Courts began experimenting with removing various rights from States' jurisdiction.

This was in direct contradiction to the promise of Rep. John Bingham of Ohio when he proposed the Fourteenth Amendment in Congress in 1866:

"I repel the suggestion made here in the heat of debate, that...this [Fourteenth Amendment]...take away from any State any right that belongs to it...The adoption of this proposed [fourteenth] amendment will take from the States no rights that belong to the States...Do gentlemen say that by so legislating [enforcing the Fourteenth Amendment] we would strike down the rights of the State? God forbid."

Unfortunately, this is exactly what activist judges began to do. With a rush of legal decisions, Federal Courts began to use the Fourteenth Amendment as a door to remove the responsibility to preserve rights out from States' jurisdiction. Federal Courts, in effect, used the Fourteenth Amendment to take the handcuffs off the Federal Government's wrists and in turn place the handcuffs on the States and the people.

In the 1957 case of *Washington Ethical Society v. District of Columbia*, Federal Judges included "ethical culture" as a religion. In the 1961 case of *Torcaso v Watkins* they included "secular humanism" as a religion. In the 1970 case of *Welsh v United States*, they included atheism as a religion.

So today, in order to not prefer one religion over another, Federal Judges have outlawed God.

In *Wallace v Jaffree*, 1985, Federal Judges not only admitted the original purpose of the First Amendment was simply to prevent the preference of one Christian denomination over another, but they also admitted to changing the meaning of the First Amendment through a "crucible of litigation":

"At one time it was thought that this right merely proscribed the preferences of one Christian sect over another...But when the underlying principle has been examined in the crucible of litigation, the Court has unambiguously concluded that the individual freedom of conscience protected by the First Amendment embraces the right to select any religious faith or none at all."

The problem with this is that it is not up to the Federal Courts to change the Constitution or the Amendments through a "crucible of litigation." If the people of the United States want to change the Constitution, they can do it by passing Amendments, as they have done twenty seven times.

Thomas Jefferson foresaw the danger of Federal Courts usurping power, writing to Mr. Hammond in 1821:

"The germ of dissolution of our federal government is in...the federal judiciary; an irresponsible body...working like gravity by night and by day, gaining a little today and a little tomorrow, and advancing its noiseless step like a thief, over the field of jurisdiction, until all shall be usurped from the States."

An example of the extent to which Federal Courts have usurped and twisted the First Amendment is Jefferson's belief in a Creator, as he wrote in the Declaration of Independence: "All men are created equal, that they are endowed by their Creator with certain unalienable Rights."

"In 2005, U.S. District Judge John E. Jones, in *Kitzmiller v. Dover Area School District,* used Jefferson's "separation" phrase to prevent students from being taught of the Creator in whom Jefferson believed: "To preserve the separation of church and state...we will enter an order permanently enjoining Defendants from maintaining the ID [Intelligent Design] Policy in any school."

Brilliant legal minds used Jefferson's words to prohibit what Jefferson believed. The American Civil "Liberties" Union uses Jefferson's phrase "separation of church and state" to remove God, despite Jefferson's warning not to remove God inscribed on the Jefferson Memorial in Washington, DC:

"God who gave us life gave us liberty. Can the liberties of a nation be secure when we have removed a conviction that these liberties are the gift of God?"

The Pew Forum on Religion & Public Life's U.S. Religious Landscape Survey (http://religions.pewforum.org/affiliations) identified the U.S. population as:

78.4% Christian, consisting of:

51.3% Evangelical/Mainline Protestant

23.9% Catholic

1.7%   Mormon

1.6%   Orthodox & other Christian

1.7%   Jewish

2.4%   Agnostic

1.6%   Atheist

1.2%   Unitarian-Universalist/Spiritual/New Age/Native

0.7%   Buddhist

0.6%   Muslim

0.4%   Hindu

0.3%   Other World Religions

12.9% Nothing in particular

The 78.4 % Christian and 1.7% Jewish give a combined total of 80.1% of U.S. citizens holding basic Judeo-Christian values, and only 1.6 % atheist.

Only 1.6 % atheist, yet they are forcing their minority views on the rest of the country!

These atheists are:

offended by prayers at graduations and football games

offended by a Cross or Star of David

offended by Christmas carols or patriotic hymns

offended by Christmas trees and menorahs

offended by the Ten Commandments or "under God" in the Pledge of Allegiance offended a teacher might hint there may be a Creator

offended a soldier said "God bless you" at a funeral

offended the Boy Scout Oath says "Do my duty to God and my country"

offended by a cross on a Veterans Memorial.

Whereas traditional Judeo-Christian belief is to forgive when offended, these atheists, when offended, sue.

A Harris Poll (2003) reported 90 percent of Americans believe in God; a Newsweek poll (2007) reported 91 percent of Americans believe in God; and a Fox News poll (2004) reported 92 percent of Americans believe in God.

It is only fitting that in a democratically elected constitutional republic, that the values of the majority of the people are reflected in the laws.

Remember Lincoln's Gettysburg Address:

"That this nation, under God, shall have a new birth of freedom—and that government of the people, by the people, for the people, shall not perish from the earth."

If the will of the majority "of the people" is not reflected in the laws, then the country has devolved into a tyranny, where the minority forces its will upon the majority. This was the situation Jefferson faced under King George III.

The current debate is not between the "religious right" and the "liberal left," it is a debate between American democracy and tyranny.

President Ronald Reagan expressed this in a radio address, February 25, 1984:

"Sometimes I can't help but feel the First Amendment is being turned on its head....The First Amendment of the Constitution was not written to protect the people from religion; that Amendment was written to protect religion from government tyranny."

Ronald Reagan said at a briefing with Midwest Editors, May 10, 1982:

"The First Amendment is to protect not government from religion, but religion from government tyranny."

Ronald Reagan addressed the Alabama State Legislature, March 15, 1982:

"To those who cite the First Amendment as reason for excluding God...may I just say: The First Amendment of the Constitution was not written to protect the people of this country from religious values; it was written to protect religious values from government tyranny."

Ronald Reagan stated in his *Salute to Free Enterprise*, January 26, 1984:

We're told that to protect the First Amendment we must expel God...Well, pardon me, but the First Amendment was not written to protect the American people from religion; the First Amendment was written to protect the American people from government tyranny.

Ronald Reagan told the National Association of Evangelicals in Orlando, Florida, March 8, 1983:

"When our founding fathers passed the First Amendment, they sought to protect churches from government interference. They never intended to construct a wall of hostility between government and the concept of religious belief itself."

Ronald Reagan stated in *Radio Address to the Nation*, September 18, 1982:

"Founding fathers...enshrined the principle of freedom of religion in the First Amendment...The purpose of that Amendment was to protect religion from the interference of government and to guarantee, in its own words, "the free exercise of religion."...The Constitution was never meant to prevent people from praying; its declared purpose was to protect their freedom to pray."

Ronald Reagan stated in a National Day of Prayer ceremony at the White House, May 6, 1982:

"Well-meaning Americans in the name of freedom have taken freedom away. For the sake of religious tolerance, they've forbidden religious practice...Thomas Jefferson once said, "Almighty God created the mind free." But current interpretation of our Constitution holds that the minds of our children cannot be free to pray to God in public schools."

Ronald Reagan asked the Ecumenical Prayer Breakfast, August 23, 1984:

"The frustrating thing is that those who are attacking religion claim they are doing it in the name of tolerance and freedom and open-mindedness. Question: Isn't the real truth that they are intolerant of religion?"

Ronald Reagan said at a ceremony for prayer in schools, September 25, 1982:

"In the last two decades we've experienced an onslaught of such twisted logic that if Alice were visiting America, she might think she'd never left Wonderland. We're told that it somehow violates the rights of others to permit students in school who desire to pray to do so. Clearly this infringes on the freedom of those who choose to pray...To prevent those who believe in God from expressing their faith is an outrage."

Ronald Reagan said in a radio address, February 25, 1984:

"Refusal to permit [religious exercises] is seen not as the realization of state neutrality, but rather as the establishment of a religion of secularism."

Ronald Reagan stated in a question & answer session, October 13, 1983:

"I hope we will also recognize the true meaning of the First Amendment. Its words were meant to guarantee freedom of religion to everyone. But I believe the First Amendment has been twisted to the point that freedom of religion is in danger of becoming freedom from religion."

Even President Bill Clinton spoke along these lines at James Madison High School, Vienna, Virginia, July 12, 1995:

"If students can wear T-shirts advertising sports teams, rock groups or politicians, they can also wear T-shirts that promote religion....Religion is too important to our history and our heritage for us to keep it out of our schools....Nothing in the First Amendment converts our public schools into religion-free zones or requires all religious expression to be left behind at the schoolhouse door."

Freedom of religion will only be protected from a big government controlled by a tyrannical minority if people remember the background of Jefferson's "separation" phrase.

Millions of people over the centuries have sacrificed much to give this generation the freedom of religion, but will it be conserved and preserved for future generations?

---

William J. Federer is author of *Backfired: A Nation Born for Religious Tolerance no Longer Tolerates Religion*. A radio and television guest, his daily *American Minute* is broadcast nationally and via the Internet. www.AmericanMinute.com. (314) 487-4395 Amerisearch, Inc., P.O. Box 20163, St. Louis, MO 63123.

# The Generous Life

## William F. High

Deep in the Ozark Mountains in southern Missouri, there is still a time and place that remains untouched by the ravages of time. The trees are so thick that you've got to hack them away if you want any sunlight to reach your little garden. But to garden, you've got to pick out thousands of rocks that seem to multiply every time a hoe hits the soil. Hunting is not a sport. It's a way of life. It's about food on the table.

It's in those hills that my own history begins. My father, Cecil Ray High, was a narrow toothpick of a man. He was the oldest of eight children. They crammed themselves in a three room log cabin that still stands to this day.

Life was hard. And, although their environment itself was hard, life was made harder by the people around them. I was named after my great grandfather William. He was a reported deadeye with a rifle. His claim to fame was having shot the ear lobe off a revenue agent out to collect taxes on his still. Later, after seeing my great grandfather in town, the revenue agent remarked, "William, look at my ear – you nearly killed me!" My great grandfather calmly replied, "If I wanted to kill you, I would aimed about two inches over."

My own grandfather, Clifford, was a harsh, mean man. His first wife died of leukemia which left him to raise eight kids on his own. By all accounts, he wasn't much good at it. Each one of those eight kids did their best to get out of those Ozark Mountains as quickly as they could.

That's where my father's journey began. At eighteen, he joined the military and soon found himself on a ship overseas to Japan. He rose to the rank of Sergeant First Class and found a career. He also found himself a wife. In post World War II Japan, there weren't many single young men left. A Japanese woman found herself with two options: marry an old Japanese man or a young American serviceman.

My mom, Kimi, was the adventurous one and chose the American serviceman. She was short and pretty – a twinkle in her eye back then, I suppose. She was never loud and vocal. By nature, the Japanese people are stoics and loyal to a fault.

It wasn't long however before their tour of service ended and they were back on a boat to America. They soon had a child in tow, then another, followed by three more. I was the fifth child in a family of six.

My dad found it hard to make ends meet on military pay, so after nine years he called it quits and went back to the working world. The journey they had together is much longer and more circuitous than these pages can contain. Suffice it to say, these were years of struggle. We were poor.

The first house I remember was a two bedroom rental. The house had no heat other than a big kerosene stove that occupied the center of our little kitchen. My mom stuffed three little kids in a single bed for warmth. We woke up on winter mornings with ice on the *inside* of the windows. Despite the lack of relative comfort, I loved that place. There were miles of hills and woods all around us, and my mom would let us explore those woods from dawn to dusk. My dad, ever the hillbilly, made sure we had cows, chickens, pigs and a huge garden. The garden, I think, was mainly for the benefit of the kids because it gave us ample opportunity to learn the distinction between weeds that needed to be pulled versus vegetables that needed to stay. I still have some of those calluses. An electrical fire ended our stay at that house.

It was after the house fire that my dad said his luck had run out. He turned to the bottle, and life never really did seem to get better. He bounced from job to job. He tried his hand at carpentry, ran a garage, did some roofing, and helped run a bar. After work, he always seemed to close out his day at the tavern with a few beers. If he came home straight from work, we kids just ran and hid. His anger was fierce until he eased some of the edge with a couple of beers.

By the time I was ten, he was a raging alcoholic and a chain smoker. He woke in the mornings with shaking hands and uncontrollable fits of coughing. The coughing grew in force until he was coughing up blood. Even an early morning beer couldn't stop the blood. After weeks of pestering, he finally went to the doctor and got the diagnosis: lung cancer.

When my mom told me that my dad had cancer, I didn't appreciate at all what it meant. After all, they told me the doctors might find some miraculous cure. I hung my hat on that and skipped off to play.

But there was no cure to be found. Eighteen months later, just one week before Christmas, December 18, 1974, my mom got the phone call that every wife and mother dreads. Her husband had passed away.

So what do you do if you are 5'1" Japanese woman with six kids to raise, no life insurance, no income, can't drive and never worked outside the home? You give your life away.

Even in the throes of my dad's cancer, my mom faced perhaps her greatest crisis. Her own mother passed away. She wanted desperately to go back to Japan and bury her mom. In fact, she'd not been back to Japan since the day she boarded that boat in 1956. But to go back meant she would have to leave my dad, the kids who needed her, not to mention we'd have to borrow from one of those high interest loan places to send her back. She didn't go.

And believe me, there were plenty of reasons to leave and not come back. My dad's alcoholism had sucked every penny from the family. His illness only worsened our finances. There were some days that a single pot of beans seemed to stretch for a week. I think every one of us kids came to hate beans and cornbread. I'm not sure how we kept the creditors away.

The alcoholism wasn't the worst of it. It was my dad's violent anger. The flashes of verbal abuse swept wide, although she bore the brunt of it.

One Christmas, the Salvation Army showed up with presents for the kids. We were that "poor family" everyone wanted to help. My dad was off at the tavern when they came. I suspect the worst part of the alcohol was knowing that she didn't have the money to buy groceries – even shoes for the kids.

A neighbor kid somehow got us signed up to play league baseball. It was my dream. Baseball was my outlet. At the time of the first game, I didn't have a pair of tennis shoes. All I had were some clunky shoes with two inch heels, and *I was the pitcher.* It was my mom who rescued me. She begged my dad to drive her to the store and let her buy me a pair of tennis shoes. Her pleading won out, and I had myself a pair of brown tennis shoes just in time for the game. I've never cherished a set of shoes as much as those.

After his passing, my mom did the only thing she knew. She got her driver's license at age forty six, and got a job. She began working in the local school cafeteria. By working at the school, she could still see us at lunchtime and be home when we got home. She was up early fixing us a brown bag lunch, and back at the stove in the evening fixing us dinner.

In looking back, those years were a period of recovery and healing. We found God's grace and sustenance. God began to visit our family. A local pastor talked to my mom about Jesus, and she trusted Him. My oldest brother had a dream too. He received a scholarship and headed off to college. There, he also found out about this person, Jesus. He came back and talked to my sister and me about this Christ.

As for myself, even at twelve and thirteen years old, I found myself immersed in the Bible. There, I met a God who I learned was my Father in a way that my earthly father could not. I was fascinated by the stories of Moses, Joshua, David & Goliath, Elijah and Elisha. From the pages of scripture, I learned to have the wings of a dream.

The strength of my mother coupled with the strength of family and faith drew us together. For the first time, we had family dinners together. And without the drain of the tavern bill there was actually a little margin. The Bible is clear that God defends the widow and is a father to the fatherless. He proved that to our family.

It's really an amazing thing. We were a family that was just dirt poor. We lived with outhouses, welfare, hand me downs, rental houses, high interest loan companies, and cars that could just barely run. But God had a different plan. My quiet little mother with her deep strength showed us that when there was a job in front of you – well, you just did it. In all of that mix of pain and struggle, God inspired a dream in each of us.

My brother wanted to coach. My sister wanted to teach. Another brother elected to become an engineer. Yet another sister chose the advertising world. All of this came from a family that no one expected anything from.

Why? What sense does one make of this? I think it starts simply with the giving. When my dad was faced with the greatest trial of his life – a house that burned down – he turned inward. His luck had run out so he turned to comfort himself. He selfishly chose the bottle instead of his faith or his family.

On the other hand, when my mom faced her own point of crisis – her mother's funeral – she chose her family. All along the way, she gave away her life and her dreams. She fought for her children even if it meant a pair of shoes. She stood beside her husband when it would've been easier to leave. She reveled in our successes – every high school graduation, every scholarship, every college degree – was hers in some measure.

One quick story deserves mentioning. When I was a high school senior, I was rated high in my class, and with it came the scholarship offers. One particular scholarship came from a women's club. They wanted to award the scholarship in person and allowed me to offer an acceptance speech. In accepting the award, I was able to tell them about my mom and her inspiration. Some of the other moms in that room that day were crying. I know that my mom was proud of me that day, but I really knew the next day. After getting home from school, she had a fresh chocolate cake waiting for me – love, spoken in Japanese culture.

It is no coincidence that today I work in the generosity world. After receiving a degree in secondary language arts education from the University of Missouri, I went on to the University of Kansas School of Law. From there, I practiced law with one of the largest law firms in the region, *Blackwell Sanders Peper Martin LLC.* That career continued with a smaller specialty firm, *Sanders Conkright & Warren.*

Eventually, after volunteering in the urban core, God showed me my calling. I'm now the President of the Servant Christian Community Foundation. There, we teach people that we are stewards or managers of God's resources. We are mere aliens on this planet who are just passing through. Our final home is heaven. With that recognition, the question is how we'll utilize the resources that God has given us.

We get to work with individuals, families, companies, ministries and churches all around the globe. Some of that work is plain and simple showing people how to give. Not long ago, I worked with a woman who, while not wealthy, wanted to do something "big" with her resources. She gave one hundred sixty five acres of virgin ground that sits adjacent to her homestead. Now she goes out on her front porch, looks at her land, and instead of land, sees people from every tribe and nation gathered at her door.

I'm just an ordinary man, but I feel I've lived a most extraordinary life. Such is the way of history. Our country was founded by a few great ideas: faith, freedom and family. It is indeed a government for the people and by the people. We stand as stewards of those great ideas. What will we do with those ideas in this day? Will we corrupt them and squander them in materialism and in lives spent on ourselves? Or will we dream the big dreams of a nation where men and women can worship freely?

I know that we can and we will accomplish the big dreams, if we remind ourselves of the lessons of the past. Our aim should not be to live for ourselves, but live to give. Such is the generous life. Such is the way of hope. All of this my mother taught me.

William F. High is the President/General Counsel of the *Servant Christian Community Foundation* (SCCF). Formerly, he practiced law with *Blackwell Sanders Peper Martin LLC.* He remains Of Counsel with *Sanders Conkright & Warren.* As a lawyer, he is licensed in the States of Kansas and Missouri and before the state and federal courts. With SCCF, he works with individuals, families, companies, ministries, churches and advisors to set up donor advised funds. These donor advised funds help people to give more simply, efficiently, and to capture existing tax advantages. SCCF is a member of the *Evangelical Council for Financial Accountability.*

# Inspired Conservatism

## Eddward T. Holliday

Inspired conservatism is hope grounded in an effective reality and faith enabling those strong in spirit to do what has never been done, and a pouring out of love transcending skin color, religion, political parties, and even socio-economic status. Indeed, conservatism embraced by a people hungry to see their world transformed becomes an inspiration. Enthusiasm for truth, knowledge, righteousness and justice emboldens those inspired by conservatism to not only talk the talk, but also to walk the walk. Like blooming flowers, an inspired conservatism reaches out to all who can see and smell, so that as long as hope endures, possibilities shall not cease; in the words of Churchill, we can never, never, never give up.

In this day and time where agents of change proliferate, we are reminded that the weather also changes. Change happens. But who should control the changing of the guard? The very word *conservative* has various meanings like keeping the *status quo*, or loathed to change. In Mississippi, where I have lived every year of my life, many African Americans discern the word conservative as a code word for racism. What is real, what is true, and what must we do to inspire a new generation to knead the dough and place yeast into the recipe for success? How can the traditional values conservatives and the African

American faith community join forces to impact our society for righteousness *and* justice? These are questions that need answers, because they have the potential to bring more than mere change.

An agent of change may ring the bell of hope, being zealous for compassion; a liberal change agent may bring good for a few people or groups, but with entirely horrible consequences for the country as a whole. We can be reminded of the story about a prison warden who had all the prisoners come out of their cells and line up in their underwear. It was a nasty prison, in a third world country, and the men had not had any new clothes for over two years. The warden said, "Men, today, every one of you is going to get a change of underwear." The men all shouted with glee. The warden told the men to remove their underwear and hold the filthy garment in their hands. "Now, hand your underwear to the man on your left." Then the warden turned around laughing and went back to his office. Just to have change does not necessarily mean that the hopes and dreams of the American people will be realized. Change; no. Transformation; yes.

A transformation comes about when an inspired conservative applies truth to debates, and presents actions that prove theories. Truly inspired conservatives can wrestle for issues on local boards, in county offices and in statewide positions. In wrestling for conservative principles, the nation as a whole experiences buds becoming blooms and positions of radical change toward the far left are not only neutralized, but effectively rendered mere ideas – ideas whose times have never come and will never see the light of day as long as inspired conservatism has a heart that beats.

A conservative movement that has grown long in the tooth has abandoned a core base of conservative ideas. A degradation has whittled away at a once bold confidence and steadfastness and left in its place an arrogance and a stubbornness. A world in which an active liberal press pounces on misdeeds and poor visionary mistakes in order to brow beat the conservatives of 2008 has placed conservatives into difficult positions. Misinformation at best, and outright perversions of truth at worst have become front page news stories. But inspired conservatives should not be afraid of the truth. We must not fear wrestling with what Americans wrestle with – it is true that after the very successful invasion of Iraq and the fall of Saddam Hussein, an arrogance and a stubbornness led to an enormous failure to discern and deal with what was happening in Iraq.

All history is a deep well that everyone has access to study. But what we know in the books doesn't mean what we learn from our surroundings is not important. President George W. Bush learned much from his family, but I am here to tell you that he is not a red blooded southerner. He may walk like he is from Texas, but that doesn't mean he really knows the South. My mother has told me stories about her grandfather during the War Between the States. I remember vividly the horror of one story. My great- grandfather was minding his own business with his rifle in hand not far from his farm when an unfortunate Yankee scout was rustling about. The Yankee started crossing a creek and just as he got to the middle in knee deep water, my great-grandfather rose up and shot the Yankee dead. What seemed to me as pure murder my mother justified by telling me what her father had told her just as his father had told him: "That Yankee had no business being in our country," which was the Confederate States of America at the time. So, if President Bush had had that southern upbringing to know that if you are invading another person's country with an army, you better darn tootin' have a plan and a back-up plan and a way to innovate, innovate, innovate. We cannot change the past, but history known will serve the inspired conservatives because we know proven principles that work. With a thorough commitment to take these principles into *every* corner of America and with a new inspiration to better know history through listening, seeing, and doing, our future looks bright. Inspired conservatives are actively engaging themselves in making their communities, their states, and their country a better place to live. If you want to see love in action go follow an inspired conservative.

Dealing with truth, the conservative movement can ask, what happened in the political arena? The Republican Party was routed in the 2006 elections after only twelve years of holding the majority in the U.S. House of Representatives and the intermittent majority in the U.S. Senate simultaneously. In efforts to build political power, conservative ideology was pushed aside in an arrogant and stubborn way. In the name of political survival, fiscal restraints were thrown out the window. Expediency led to a weakened conservatism within the Republican Party and therefore a lack of leadership in the entire conservative movement.

As many conservatives bask in the memory of President Reagan's term, they speak nostalgically of the Reagan Revolution. My friends, there would have never been a Reagan revolution if it were not for Democrats like Senator John C. Stennis and U.S. Representative Sonny Montgomery—both of Mississippi. Reagan effectively used bipartisanship to get his agenda through the U.S. Congress. Without the support of conservative Democrats, President Reagan would never have been an effective agent of government transformation. His policies caused a transformation in thinking and governmental behavior – not just change. The world was transformed with the Gipper at the helm. Even though his critics were many and their rhetoric sometimes vicious, President Reagan took his vision of transformation and with his leadership, he crafted it into reality. And our country and our world became better places for life to be lived more freely and more abundantly.

Today we need an inspired conservatism that thinks outside the box. We need not be limited to NASCAR fans or conservative action groups. Inspired conservatives are more than one religion, one race, one focus group, and one region of the country. If an inspired conservatism has principles that propel a society to greatness, then it will draw all kinds of people to its cause. Inspiration of conservatism in the twenty first century must seek leaders from all peoples and groups. Ideas such as inspired conservatives hold cannot be limited, rather they must be unleashed so that there is an intentional, vibrant effort anew to seek the African American faith community, to seek the Hispanic community, and to reach out to those who share a vision like Jefferson who said that government governs best when it governs the least. And, yet, we have failed to lead by example. We have failed to make plain just how the free enterprise system can go into the inner cities and the rural blights and transform a community in despair into a community of hope. That, my friends is the difference between merely conservative and an inspired conservatism. We are learning, but we have not arrived as of yet. But we will.

Inspired conservatism should resonate throughout all communities with a hope of proven policies that melt down the theories of the far left agenda. An inspired conservatism relies on what Dr. Martin Luther King, Jr. might call the underlying moral principle – that there are some things that cannot be legislated, they must be lived. Jesus said, "Do unto others as you would have them do unto you." He also said, "Love your neighbor as yourself." The horror of the Columbine school shootings, and all other selfish shooting atrocities since then, are the anti-Jesus declarations. Dr. King in all his courage to live free no matter what the cost, would have today been horrified that with all our advances in breaking down racial barriers. We have failed in our moral objectives as a culture. Indeed, Dr. King in one of his influential sermons told how we must go back before we could ever move forward. He preached that in all our technological advances, we as a society must go back to the Judeo-Christian principles on which our nation was founded. He told how when Jesus was left in Jerusalem as a boy, Mary and Joseph had to return to the city to discover Jesus – before moving forward again toward their home in Nazareth. Today, we have conservatives who need to return and discover what they have left behind, so that we as a movement can be *inspired* conservatives, and we as a nation can move forward to obtain the greatness that is the destiny of a country brimming with hope, promises and ideas. The people of the world long and ache to see such an America in action.

One failure of the conservative movement today is its inability, thus far, to attract large numbers of African Americans. The conservatives of today can be paralleled to the gay and lesbian activists. Many in the gay and lesbian lifestyles have bought into the myth that they were just born that way. Many in the conservative movement have bought into the myth that they do not need the African American community. Just as the gay and lesbian community would rather have those who have unwanted same sex attractions imprisoned to these desires, there are those in the conservative movement who find it easier to send money to African nations than to work with African Americans in their own cities. But, the future of the conservative movement's strength will be proportional to its ability to intentionally reach out and secure large numbers of African Americans and Hispanics.

Though few conservatives like to admit their weaknesses, when it comes to racial issues, there are many. There are no white sheeted Klansmen terrifying people in the dark, but there is the inability to see the subtle racism that has taken a cultural backseat as conservative ideas are defined, tested, and crafted for public consumption. These subtle mannerisms come in different subconscious disguises. I mention them here not for malicious purposes, but to correct and to edify conservatives for the future, to inspire the true conservatives. The mental picture of equal access, for all ideas at the conservative table, must become a reality. By this I mean that conservatives should welcome new ideas to establish and develop new relationships within the African American community. Intentional avenues should be established so that true friendships can develop within all communities on the national, state, and local level. Just like conservatives do on other issues, we can always agree to disagree on some subjects, but without relationships, we will be destined to thinking only within a small box. America and the world deserves much better than small-box-thinking conservatives. If every conservative becomes inspired to intentionally seek African American and Hispanic contacts, our nation will become a better country. If inspired conservatives become agents for transformation, our country will become so unbelievably blessed that we cannot imagine the enormous economic consequences and the immeasurable joy coming from a culture and society that respects life, marriage, and from the healthy transitions resonating from healthy governmental policies.

We are in a momentous period of history. Our country is making decisions now that will affect this nation and this world for decades to come. There are liberal "hate crime" bills that seek to become law; they will stifle free speech. Indeed, we can say unashamedly that the radical gay and lesbian activists are actively pursuing the establishment of the *Jim Crow* laws for the twenty-first century. Freedom of speech must be defended. Marriage as a traditional, stable institution that has benefited societies around the globe for millennia is now on the ropes in the United States. If conservatives can not be inspired to protect traditional marriage then we will never be able to provide the strategic ideas that will fuel the economic engine needed for a prosperous people.

I believe that our country has moved forward in many points of freedom. In 2008 we find a forty year cycle coming to completion. It has been forty years since Dr. King was assassinated. It has been forty years since the radical left agenda captured the heart of the Democratic national leadership, and it has been forty years since Ronald Reagan was in the middle of his first term as governor of California. I feel that our nation and the conservative movement have come out of Egypt, but we have been wandering in the desert now for forty years. It is time to cross the Jordan River and to take the Promised Land! Inspired conservatives step forward!!

Dr. Edward T. Holliday owns his own dentistry practice in Tupelo, Mississippi. He is the author of the book, 21$^{st}$ Century Great Awakening. Dr. Holliday is married to his wife Leslie and has four wonderful children.

# Conservative Family Values: A Biblical Perspective

## Pastor Andrew Jackson

I believe that one of the greatest threats in this country today is the destruction of the family. To say this is almost an understatement, in the light of the recent decision of the ruling Justices in Massachusetts and then again in California.

Both those courts, with arrogant self-conceit based on a twisted idea of compassion, have decided that they and they alone among all human societies have the correct understanding of marriage. They have decided that sexuality has no relationship to marriage.

The truth of God is this: God established three basic units for the survival of society. And not only for its mere survival, but for a successful society.

*One of these basic units is the church.* A society without God crumbles, and quickly. The swift fall of the atheistic regimes in the twentieth century are enough proof for those with eyes to see.

*One of these basic units is the government.* But the government cannot create a strong society, only one that is secure from enemies outside or civil strife inside. In fact, as any government gets stronger, its people atrophy and grow weaker. Look at the strong governments of western Europe where the spiritual, intellectual and economic muscle is wasting away under strong bureaucrats.

And one of these basic units is the family.

No matter how great a government, or how well entrenched a "Christian" tradition may be, a society is no greater than its families. And families are created by human beings with family values established by God. I believe in the family values that God Himself set forth in the Bible.

Allow me to share just a few of them.

First of all, God created Adam and Eve – not Adam and Steve. He said that there should be one husband for one wife, for life. He said that marriage should only be between a man and a woman. Period.

Same-sex marriage, adultery, and fornication will simply destroy a society. Every society in history has protected families by regulating sexual activity. Sometimes the strictures were strong, and sometimes they were weaker, but in every society they exist. They exist because the committed heterosexual sexual relationship is the very heart of marriage, and marriage is the heart of any society.

## Someone Might Ask: "Where's the proof?"

For those who respect what the Bible says, I have already given it: God's original description of creation, one man, one woman, for life.

For those who aren't happy with that, then I suppose it is like asking for proof that green isn't the same thing as orange. You can point to it, and you can call attention to it, but if a person cannot see the difference for themselves, it is because of a perversion in one of three places: their mind, their eye or their honesty.

As I mentioned it, every society sees the need to protect the family from sexual deviation and unrestricted sexual license. They don't do it because of a text book or a scientific study. They do it because, in fact, it is the very same as the ability to tell one color from another: it is obvious if you haven't been corrupted by personal desire or political indoctrination.

In the words of J. Budziszewski: it is something that a normal human being simply cannot not know. It is part of the law of God written on the heart of every human being.

Who cannot know that the family is the training ground for solid citizens? For instance, when the Bible mentions that we as parents should train up a child in the way they should go, it isn't merely stating a simple command from the Word of God; it's clearly a biblical principle that's workable.

God has not left the world without a witness in the most fundamental areas of basic morality. This includes the home and family. I believe that God has a destiny and a purpose for every person who comes into this world. I also believe that we can find our destiny and purpose in the Word of God.

For example, according to 2 Peter 3:9, God is not willing that any should perish, but all should come to repentance. He wants every person to be saved and not lost. If that is true, then He has not left it up to a handful of arrogant men in the black-robed legal priesthood to announce in their 'wisdom' that marriage is not what every human society has always known that it is.

Furthermore, He says to us that we must trust in the Lord with all our heart, and lean not upon our understanding, that if we acknowledge Him in all our ways, He will direct our paths (Proverbs 3:5-6). That being so, He has not left all humanity in ignorance for thousands of years about the basic structure of human birth, death and daily life: the home.

Those who would destroy our homes begin by deciding that there is no divine purpose for our lives. This is, obviously, contrary to biblical revelation.

He says in Matthew 6:33 to seek first the Kingdom of God and His righteousness, and all other things will be added to us. God, Who is our Creator, knows the purpose for which He created us. If we are to know why we are here, and how to be while here, then we must go to the one Who created us – God.

In a nutshell, you and I were created to bring glory and honor to God. But what do homosexuals believe about bringing honor and glory to God? What do their lives say about it? What would they teach the children who were shackled to them under a mindless foster 'parent' system?

I learned my family values, where else, in my family!

My mother was a Christian, my father was not. But my father had enough respect for God to allow my mother to set the values which he enforced. The rules were that we had family prayer, Bible reading and we went to church at least twice a week.

My mother was arguably the greatest influence in my life. I wonder what some foster child chained to a homosexual 'couple' will have to say about their greatest influence.

I became a born-again Christian at the age of thirteen. The religious principles and values that were instilled in me during my youth have greatly shaped my life. My mother had some very strict religious views. As I grew older, I gained a tremendous appreciation for my religious training. As a result, I believe I am a better person in Christ.

But I also learned how to take my place is society from my family.

I grew up on a farm where I chopped and picked cotton. I bailed hay and milked cows. I raised and even killed hogs, all of which allowed me to learn responsibility at an early age. I wasn't raised in a home where the 'parents' couldn't even participate in the creation of a child, only then to be held up as 'models' of what responsibility was like.

I was the second oldest of eight children. I graduated from high school when I was seventeen, and then got married about a year later. My wife, Lottie, gave me six wonderfully talented children, three sons and three daughters.

Through God's blessing of our married sexuality we participated in the very creation of these children, which bonded us to them and they to us. We modeled responsibility and we modeled commitment. Neither can be modeled in a homosexual relationship regardless if police-state enforcers paste the word marriage on it.

For the next few years, my wife and I continued to pursue our education, particularly in the medical field. Consequently, I spent ten years as a research associate at Northwestern University in Chicago and the following ten years at the University of Tennessee. Lottie, on the other hand, spent years working as an operating room technician at a medical facility in Chicago.

But we didn't need to have our education tell us that God's plan for the family is not only normal, it is without parallel. Any changing is perversion. Any perversion is weakening. Any weakening will destroy the society that our homes are part of.

But family values are not only about family.

They are also about loving and serving society at large. During that particular time, I felt a strong calling to go into the ministry. Such a calling eventually led to me obtaining both Bachelors and Masters degrees in Theology from Friends International University in California.

My wife, always instrumental in my life, likewise eventually received a certificate in Biblical Studies from the Charles Harrison Mason Bible College.

In the meantime, God blessed me through establishing Faith Temple Church (currently known as Faith Temple Ministries Church) in Memphis, Tennessee. I established this with the commitment of my wife, six children, and two other adults. In fact, my wife and family have remained an integral part of the ministry since its inception in 1969.

The ministry has grown tremendously over the past thirty eight years. I attribute the phenomenal growth not only to God's favor, but also to the input and contributions by my family. My family taught biblical family values in the context of a normal human family organized as God created it, and functioning as God designed it.

We raised our children in a manner similar to the way we were raised. We practiced and taught them Biblical principles and family values. We taught them to make Jesus the center of their lives, to treat people the way they wanted to be treated and to get an education. And the point ought to be obvious: you cannot teach what you do not live, especially in the context of your family!

How is it possible for those whose life-style is based on unlimited license possibly model self-sacrifice, generosity and love? A little known fact is that while practicing homosexuals have a far higher than average income (why not, since they pursue careers without the burden of family obligations), they contribute virtually no money to charitable causes other than political action groups.

Well, as a result of traditional family training (and her own good judgment), Patricia, our eldest child, is a teacher in the Memphis Public School System. She also works with her husband, Aaron, who pastors the Rising Sun Outreach Church.

As a result of traditional family training (and his own good judgment) Andrew, Jr. our second-oldest child, retired from Delta Airlines a couple of year ago and pastors the West Irving Church of God In Christ in Dallas, Texas. He and his family reside in Bedford, Texas.

And then there is Ivory, arguably the most diverse of all of my children. As a result of traditional family training (and his own good judgment), he has committed himself in the ministry. Having retired from Kroger, one of the largest food chains in the country, he and his wife, Lisa, are currently serving with me in the ministry as Youth Directors. Ivory also serves as Faith Temple's Second Assistant Pastor.

Derrick, a co-founder of the Jackson School of Music, is the chief musician for our church. Both our family values and his own good judgment has long been evident. He traveled with the late Bishop G. E. Patterson for seven years as his personal organist.

Like Derrick, Barbara is co-founder and chief executive officer of the Jackson School of Music. In addition to serving as vice-president of the international music department for COGIC, she is the First Assistant pastor and Minister of Music at our church. And where would she be without traditional family values, and the resulting good judgment?

Our youngest child, Sharon, is married and has two children. She is the corporate secretary, choir directress and, most notably, the praise and worship leader at Faith Temple. The good judgment instilled by good family values are obvious for anyone who does not close his eyes.

Now let me hasten to say that our family is by no means perfect, nor do we consider ourselves to be the ideal family. There is no such thing. We have had our share of challenges and will continue to have them. Nevertheless, we are a closely connected family. We consistently work together, we help one another, and we help share each other's burden. Most importantly, my wife and I taught them to trust God. Because, after all, it is His strength that is made perfect in weakness.

I firmly believe the time my wife and I spent with them when they were children has had a positive impact on their lives.

We took them on vacations at least twice a year, made it a point to visit their schools regularly, encouraged them to be the best they could be and, most importantly, we prayed with and for them on a regular basis.

I suppose that the robed legal reformers of California and Massachusetts wouldn't recognized the value of this traditional committed love.

My family believes in greatness, but only the kind of greatness that comes through service. Service is taught best by the greatest institution upon the face of the earth – the family.

From the family comes the government. From the family comes the church. Good families produce good government, good churches and good societies.

With this in mind, allow me to offer you words of encouragement and hope.

Fleshly-minded reformers who litigate and legislate against our families want to say that family failures prove that the family has failed. But they are wrong again.

You may feel as if you are a failure, that you have failed your family, or that your family is a failure. Well, failure is a part of life. Failure is a part of success. And success is simply when preparation meets opportunity. So it's not over until you give up or quit. Winners are just ex-losers who refuse to quit. My family is made of ex-losers who refuse to quit. You are important to God. Your family is important to God.

So you see, God's purpose for you and your family haven't, in any way, been canceled because of your failures. God is a God of many chances. You have another chance to fulfill your purpose for which God created you. The best way that this can be done is through Jesus Christ. In fact, it is Jesus Who says that "without Me, you can do nothing."

So remember this: the family was God's idea. The family that prays together stays together. But the nation that refuses to stand by the family is cutting itself off from its ultimate source of strength. Our nation, like any individual, can live for a while with cancer. But if it doesn't work to destroy the cancer, like any individual, the cancer will works its magic, black magic. This is nothing less than God's justice.

Pastor Andrew Jackson is founder and Senior Pastor of Faith Temple Ministries Church of God in Christ in Memphis, Tennessee. He is the past chairman for the Memphis Chapter of the Pentecostal Charismatic Churches of North America (PCCNA). He is married to his wife Lottie and has six beautiful children.

# Shedding the Labels and Boxes: Embracing the Truth

### Dr. Alveda C. King
### with Elizabeth Stoner

*Galatians 4:16 – "Am I therefore become your enemy, because I tell you the truth?"*

In preparing this chapter, I was constantly plagued with the burden that accompanies bearing the conservative label. I find that I resist being painted into a corner and confined in a box that is currently labeled as "conservative." The labels of Conservative and Liberal are just as dangerous and misleading as any other labels. They are ambiguous and subjective so they don't convey a clear meaning. Then when they are attributed to or appointed to a person or a group, an instant division occurs. Labels prohibit people who often share common beliefs on certain issues from standing together with others who believe some of what the first group believes, but not everything.

The following definitions should clearly and easily distinguish the group labeled "liberal" from the group labeled "conservative."

Liberal – "favorable to progress or reform, as in political or religious affairs"

Progress – "a movement toward a goal or to a further or higher stage"

Conservative – "having the power or tendency to conserve; preserve"

Reform – "the improvement or amendment of what is wrong, corrupt, unsatisfactory, etc.: social reform; spelling reform, to put an end to (abuses, disorders, et cetera)"

Conserve – "to prevent injury, decay, waste, or loss of"

Preserve – "to keep alive or in existence; make lasting: to preserve our liberties as free citizens, to keep safe from harm or injury, protect or spare"

Yet, we find that even the dictionary definitions overlap, causing one to wonder if liberal means conservative and vice versa. For instance, some stand for protecting the lives of our children at *all* stages of life, beginning with the conception of the forty six chromosomes, and ending at natural death. Pro-lifers are neither preventing nor denying life, liberty and justice; pro-lifers are not holding back liberty of life. So pro-life can be both liberal and conservative. Oh what fun it is to play the label game!

My friend Elizabeth Stoner explains the tragedy of labels this way:

We have driven a lot of cars in our day, some new, some used and some just mere relics of what once was. At one point when our money was low, we purchased a vehicle that came with those wonderful outdated political bumper stickers. There is nothing like running around with a Carter bumper sticker when George Bush Sr. is in office. So, being naïve as to the tenacity with which these labels are designed to adhere to the surface they are placed on, I figured I could apply some elbow grease and chemicals to get the label off. The next morning after breakfast I went forth, armed with my rubber gloves, scruggie, soapy water and pure ammonia.

First I applied the soapy water liberally and then tried to scrub through the label with a scruggie – no give. Then I applied pure ammonia, which loosened only the congestion in my head. Next I went into the kitchen for a razor blade, figuring I could gently get the edges to come loose and then ease the rest of the label off. After about twenty minutes of trying this, the only thing that gave were my ruined rubber gloves, which now had so many bits missing, that I had to go get another pair. While I was inside I grabbed an extension cord and a hair dryer, assuming that if I heated the sticker, it might come loose. I was able to get bits and pieces of it off, but never the whole thing. It now looked worse than when I started. So, having only paid one hundred fifty dollars for the car, including duct tape on the seats, I dried the chrome bumper and neatly covered the offending sticker with more gray duct tape. I called the morning a "wash."

As I sat on the porch, sipping my iced tea, rocking in my chair, a light suddenly came on in my mind. I realized the morning had not been a futile effort at all. There were scores of lessons to be learned from that old bumper sticker.

## First, Labels Stick

When we Christians label one another, be it our children, our spouse or our fellow man, the labels have a tendency to stick. The more we use them, the greater the bond between man and label becomes. We get tired and frustrated that our toddlers have not yet learned to see what is obvious to us. Suddenly we call them stupid, or dumb, or some other barb that sticks in their minds and begins to grow. We feel insecure or frightened so we brand groups and organizations portraying them as the enemy. Then wonder why we cannot work or live together in harmony. We view religions, creeds, ethnic groups and even socio-economic groups as either acceptable or not by criteria that are often based on fear, insecurity, lies and sin. Then, after we have wrongfully judged them, we label them with hateful, demeaning, divisive names that stick. Later, when we find a common cause, we struggle to unite, often failing because of distrust, deep wounds, and divisions these labels have bred within us. Labels stick.

## Second, Labels Are Hard to Remove

Sadly, we often realize our mistake after the toddler has become a young adult. He's grown up hearing us berate him in anger with labels. Year by year we ingrained a false understanding of himself into the fiber of his heart and character until finally, when we wake up and see what we have done, the damage is deeply rooted. It will not easily be removed.

The economy is a problem, yet another war needs to be addressed, poverty is rampant and spreading. As a society we need to come together to solve these problems, but the labels are stuck. We don't trust each other. We don't see each other in the light of what we can become, preferring the archaic and hateful labels we have grown up to embrace. So our collaborations are weak when we need them to be strong, and we find the ability to stand together for a good cause difficult or nearly impossible. It should be so easy.

We want to trust each other, but the labels are sticking.

We want to be unafraid, but the labels are sticking.

We want to forgive, but the labels are bound deep in our hearts.

We want to unite, but the labels just will not give.

Labels are hard to remove.

## Third, Patch, Move On And Heal

Sometimes we just have to put a patch on it and try to move forward in hopes that time will heal. The patch is not pretty. The beauty of the sparkling polished chrome will be forever marred, but gradually, over time, things change. The bumper gets old, peeling and rusting. Then suddenly a duct tape patch doesn't stand out so much. But it takes a lot of time and sadly, while we can move forward, there will always be damage, to some degree, left behind.

Labels prevent us from loving one another as God has commanded us to do. Labels inhibit us from doing unto others as we would have them to unto us. Labels hinder us from allowing the fruits of the Spirit to flow from our hearts to those around us. Labels ostracize people who are created in God's image. They cause us to do what God says is foolish – judging ourselves by others rather than by the law of God. Labels impede movement toward the unity, peace and harmony for which our families, communities, nation and world are pleading.

Christians must avoid labels at all cost. After all, the bumper stickers we are applying daily adhere to human hearts, not to mere cars or buildings. The bond and the subsequent damage runs deep and affects not only individuals but families, communities and nations, generation after generation. The use of labels in our lives *must* stop – immediately. I hope you remember this thought every time you see a bumper sticker."

After reading and re-reading Elizabeth's analogy, I realized why it took so long for me to write this chapter. I was waiting for her to journal this truth in writing. Labels are divisive, and boxes are restrictive, which is why I resist the label of "conservative."

The practice of accepting and assigning labels and boxes is another form of assigning separatism to the human race. This practice is deceptive and dangerous. We are one human race, not separate races, not separate classes divided by skin color. There is no red or black, white, brown or yellow race. There is one human race with ethnic distinctions. So when we put people in a "color box," we begin to discriminate, which is sin!

Another consequence of labeling and boxing is restricting God given gifts that emerge in people we have stereotyped. For example, can an accountant not also be a poet? Can a scientist not also be a great cook? When we label people according to our understanding of their gifts and talents, we leave no room for God's creativity to abundantly burst forth in multiple streams. I have a friend who is a real estate and investment genius. Yet, he is a wonderful composer and music producer. Some people seriously tell him that his music is a nice hobby, but that he should stick to one thing. How sad!

In the beloved community, so named by my uncle, Dr. Martin Luther King, Jr., labels, boxes and separate races don't exist. To close by returning to the initial thought, the conservative label is not a badge of honor. It is a state of being, a cry for liberty in a world that is hungry for truth. Let us pray that we move on from labels and boxes into a higher place where love abounds.

Dr. Alveda C. King founded King for America, Inc. "to assist people in enriching their lives spiritually, personally, mentally and economically." She is the daughter of the late slain civil rights activist Rev. A. D. King and his wife Naomi Barber King. Alveda is the grateful mother of eight children and she is a doting grandmother.

During the more than half century of her life, Alveda has worked towards her purpose of glorifying God in the earth by accomplishing many goals. Currently, Alveda is a minister of the Gospel of Jesus Christ, serving as Director of African American Outreach for Gospel of Life, headed up by Father Frank Pavone of Priests for Life. She also consults with the Africa Humanitarian Christian Fellowship, founded by her mentor, Pastor Allen McNair of Believers' Bible Christian Church in Atlanta, Georgia.

She is a former college professor, holding the Masters of Arts degree in Business Management from Central Michigan University. Her undergraduate studies in journalism and sociology helped her to become a published author, the most popular works being her best selling books *The Sons of Thunder: The King Family* and *I Don't Want Your Man, I Want My Own*. This inspirational collection of Christian testimonies is used at conferences and workshops around the world. Alveda's Doctorate of Laws was conferred by Saint Anslem College. She has served as a Senior Fellow of the Alexis de Tocqueville Institute. She has also served on the boards and committees of numerous organizations, including the *Silent No More Awareness Campaign, Coalition Of African American Pastors,* and the *Judeo-Christian Coalition For Constitutional Restoration.* She also served in the Georgia State House of Representatives, and is an accomplished actress.

# The Ten Commandments as The Root of American Culture

## James Linzey, D.D.

The Declaration of Independence and the Gettysburg Address are two of the most famous and widely circulated vision statements ever composed. Together they are the spiritual constitution of the United States, and at the time they were written, each served a great purpose. Both documents, poetic enough to be literature, mingle the controversy of the time with the broad outlook of a noble appeal for the dignity and rights of Americans. And both are reasoned enough to carry conviction yet inspire enthusiasm among followers. They are empowering statements that have impacted our nation for many years. They have established a system of ethics and morality to govern our nation.

Moral Leadership has always had a place in our country. We may not see it for periods of time as we look around and think that all leadership around us is corrupt. However, there has always been a remnant of those leaders with strong moral codes of behavior who have stood their ground for the right way of dealing with fellow human beings. Some of those moral leaders have been national or state leaders—presidents, congressmen, senators, state officers, city leaders. Others have been smaller leaders—church deacons, managers of work places, clerks at community offices, privates in the army. But whether in a large pool or a small pool, these leaders have reminded us that morality exists and that it is important to keep our own moral code in good repair, to behave to others as we would like them to behave to us.

Many organizational leaders believe it is possible to violate ethical and moral standards of action and still profit from their business and their clientele. However, most such actions end up hurting the businesses and alienating the employees/followers. It all comes down to right and wrong. Leaders cannot continue to violate the right and wrong of the society in which they work if they want to continue to gain in their businesses. As Bob Allen, executive of AT&T said, "You can't win out in the long run by . . . taking short-run advantage that is ethically or morally wrong. You err on the side of being absolutely pure. I do business with almost anybody as long as they are willing to negotiate on moral and ethical terms" (From a student interview conducted with Allen, qtd. in Haas, 157).

How does this kind of moral integrity relate to or connect to leadership in general in the United States? The recent debate over the legitimacy of hanging copies of the Ten Commandments in schoolrooms and courtrooms illustrates the problem in our nation with moral living and moral leadership. The Ten Commandments from the Bible were originally accepted as the basis for the founding of our nation. Our Founding Fathers referred to them and used them as a basis for the moral essentials of our country. In fact, James Madison, the father of the Constitution, said, "We have staked the entire future of the American civilization not upon the power of government but upon the capacity of the individual to govern himself, control himself, and sustain himself according to the Ten Commandments of God" (Scarborough 1).

Many people believe the Ten Commandments have no place in our public lives—certainly not in schools and courts. They believe, suddenly and only recently, that putting the Ten Commandments on the wall in a classroom or courtroom in the United States is a radical, dangerous attempt to overthrow our American freedoms. In fact, some are incensed that the "Christians" in this country are trying to take over the founding documents by claiming biblical references and heritage when such does not exist. However, a look at the original documents of our founding will prove without a doubt that the founding Fathers deliberately worked from the premise of the morality of the Holy Bible, especially from the Ten Commandments. Many seem to have forgotten that George Washington, in his farewell address as leader of the United States of America, said, "It is impossible to govern this country or any country in the world rightly without a belief in God and the Ten Commandments" (Scarborough 2).

Because some people today are not familiar with the Ten Commandments (aside from hearing the controversy about them in the newspapers), perhaps a short review of what they are and what they intend to do would be helpful.

The Ten Commandments as given in Exodus 20 can be abbreviated to these:

1. You shall have no god before Me (the Judeo-Christian Lord God),

2. You shall not make idols in any form or worship idols in any form,

3. You shall not misuse the name of the Lord (in swearing),

4. You shall keep the Sabbath day holy,

5. You shall honor your father and mother,

6. You shall not murder,

7. You shall not commit adultery,

8. You shall not steal,

9. You shall not lie (or give any kind of false testimony), and

10. You shall not covet anything that belongs to anyone else.

These ten "commands" are statements of the way to act if we would be moral people. Notice that only two of the ten have anything directly to say about God (#1 and #3, though #2 could be implied to do so as well). People mistakenly think that the Ten Commandments are all about religion or worshipping God. Not so.

They are about living a decent moral life in community with other people. They are about being human and treating others as human beings too. They have to do with every person's relationship to every other person. We cannot violate these standards of behavior in our relationships to those around us and still call ourselves moral beings or even human beings at all as we were intended to be. This is common good behavior—for leaders as well as for followers.

It is interesting to note that one can follow or keep all of the Ten Commandments with no outside help—religious or otherwise. It is certainly possible for all of us, if we use our best judgment and discipline, to obey all of these on our own—by our own ability. In other words, we are all capable of being moral human beings. We don't always choose to act accordingly, however. It is much easier to lie sometimes than to be the moral person who tells the truth. Our society often excuses an addict for his drug habit, giving him the benefit of not being able to help himself. But that same society has different standards when it comes to lying, cheating, and living in any other immoral way. Society wants to blame our moral failures on our inability to keep such stringent demands from a stern God. However, notice that God asks nothing of us that we are not able to do ourselves.

We live in community with other human beings, and God knows that for the community to survive, certain rules or laws must be in effect. These ten "rules" (or "commands" for living in community) that God gives are the basic core of survival. Without them, the community is destroyed.

There is another way of looking at these commandments though. In the New Testament, the part of the Bible that tells of Christianity and life after Jesus came to earth, we are told how to transfer the commandments of action given in the Old Testament (the ten things we must do to survive in community) to commandments of attitude. Moral beings live by attitude more than by actions. How easy it is for actions to measure up to some sort of code of behavior while the mind and heart are bitter, resentful, angry, hateful, and feeling just the opposite of what the bodily actions indicate. In other words, we can politely say, "I'm sorry" when we are coerced to do so by our parents or teachers, while at the same time hatefully saying in our hearts, "I'm glad I kicked your face in."

There may often be a huge discrepancy between action and attitude. Jesus deals with this discrepancy in His teachings on the Ten Commandments. In the book of Matthew, chapter 5, Jesus refocuses the Commandment from the action of murder to the attitude of murder by telling us that murder is not just the action of killing someone, but it is the attitude of being really angry with our brothers and neighbors (vv. 21-26). He tells us that adultery is not simply taking someone not our spouse (an action), but it is looking at someone lustfully (an attitude) whether we take that person or not: "anyone who looks at a woman lustfully has already committed adultery with her in his heart" (Matt. 5:28).

Moral living, then, is based not simply on the physical keeping of the law or of the Ten Commandments of the Old Testament, but it is keeping the intent of the law in our hearts and minds. It is being willing to live according to the moral context behind the laws rather than trying to get around or avoid their meaning. If we want to live morally pure lives, we must keep our bodies and minds in control. The Ten Commandments ask us to do that. And we can readily see that whether we are speaking of the actions or the attitudes, living in community requires that we follow basic commands of getting along with others and valuing the lives of others.

Why, then, is it so difficult for people to abide by the Ten Commandments? Most of us would agree that we don't want others to lie, cheat, kill, commit adultery with our spouses, or covet our possessions. Why don't we keep the commands ourselves if we want others to do so? The basic problem is with Command #1. If we truly love the Lord God first—put no other gods or possessions or people before Him—then we can keep the rest of the commands with little trouble. But most people like to put themselves first, or put their jobs or careers or possessions or money or fame or health first. Those things or people who are most important to us are the ones who become our "gods" or "idols" (as mentioned in Command #2). Because we don't acknowledge God first, we have no reason to follow the rest of the commands—there is no longer any social, physical, political or economic reason to keep the Ten Commandments. No one will pay us to keep them. The only reason for keeping them is the moral one. And if it suits us to lie or violate any of the other nine commands, we do so. Once we break one command, it is very easy to break all the rest of them. We may not actually physically kill a person, but we will allow ourselves to hate someone to the extent that we almost wish that person dead—the same as committing murder.

Because our nation has not kept the code of morality alive in its dealings with the American people, the people of our nation in turn do not keep moral conduct toward the nation. Our leaders break the Ten Commandments every day in the political life, the social life, the physical life of our nation. No wonder they do not want the Ten Commandments on the walls of our Courts and public buildings—the reminder of those standards brings too much guilt and shame on the actions taking place in those buildings. The people of our nation know the leaders lie and cheat, so the people see no reason they should not follow suit. If the big leaders get away with it, why shouldn't the small everyday people also get away with it? So the moral code goes out with the garbage and the morality of the nation degenerates to selfishness and trying to get away with more than the other guy gets away with.

How, then, does this moral stance of a nation relate to the morality of leadership? The concepts in those commands apply to all phases of life and all areas of relationships. A successful leader will not continue to be successful if he/she begins to lie, steal, cheat, or murder those who get in the way of success. Though our country's moral position is not what it used to be in the early days of our founding, we do not individually want to follow a leader who is known to be dishonest and undependable. So whether or not a leader claims any religious affiliation, we want that leader to live according to the rules of living in community. We want that leader to be trustworthy and dependable. As we look later at the most desired traits of a leader, we will notice that many of those traits have to do with the moral character of that leader rather than with his economic or social stance or abilities. And moral character, of course, is closely associated with the Ten Commandments.

Perhaps the most important connection between the Ten Commandments and leadership is simply that the Commandments do deal with relationships between people. Robert D. Dale, in his book on leadership, creates the ten commandments of leaders. His commandments are aimed primarily at the leadership of teams, but they are applicable to all leaders as well because he considers the leader in relationship to the people that leader leads. Though Dale labels his list as "commandments," he also calls them ten principles to follow in team building. The first five focus on concerns with people, and the second five focus on production issues. These two parts of leadership must be maintained in balance—people as well as production. Here are Dale's commandments:

1. Develop personal ownership of your team's life and work. People support what they help create.

2. Surface expectations. Everyone expects something from

the groups he/she is involved with. Recognize there are different personal agendas and work together.

3. Create a "we" climate. A "we" climate comes when leaders take responsibility for failures and share the successes.

4. Recognize relational roles in teams. A broad range of relational roles will exist in any group.

5. Do team repair. Groups need maintenance to run smoothly.

6. Define the core mission of your organization. No team can function productively without a clear vision of its task.

7. Identify the formal task groups you work with. There may be an overlap of members' responsibilities. Note the overlapping members and be aware of when to change hats. Select the right hat for each occasion.

8. Develop team task descriptions. Efficient job descriptions cut down on gaps and overlaps.

9. Monitor task roles on the team. Having some who can fill several roles aids the whole team.

10. Learn to manage meetings. Guiding a process in meetings is better than controlling people (pp. 100-104).

Any organization is made up of a wide variety of teams. Some teams work together better than others. The goal of a leader is to put together all the diverse gifts, roles, and resources of a group of people and have them function for a common cause. When this is done, the leader has succeeded.

*In a kind of parallel to the idea of the Ten Commandments, James Kouzes and Barry Posner, authors of The Leadership Challenge: How to Keep Getting Extraordinary Things Done in Organizations,* have coined what they call the "Ten Commitments of Leadership." These 10 commitments are sub-headings under their five fundamental practices of exemplary leadership and serve as the basis for learning to lead. Their five fundamental practices of exemplary leadership are these: Challenging the Process, Inspiring a Shared Vision, Enabling Others to Act, Modeling the Way, and Encouraging the Heart. The Ten Commitments, then, which are sub-points of those five, are as follows:

1. Search out challenging opportunities to change, grow, innovate, and improve.

2. Experiment, take risks, and learn from the accompanying mistakes.

3. Envision an uplifting and ennobling future.

4. Enlist others in a common vision by appealing to their values, interests, hopes, and dreams.

5. Foster collaboration by promoting cooperative goals and building trust.

6. Strengthen people by giving power away, providing choice, developing competence, assigning critical tasks, and offering visible support.

7. Set the example by behaving in ways that are consistent with shared values.

8. Achieve small wins that promote consistent progress and build commitment.

9. Recognize individual contributions to the success of every project.

10. Celebrate team accomplishments regularly (17-18).

Notice that in both lists—whether commitments or commandments—the key focus is on the people involved. If a leader ignores the people who are following, then that leader might as well count on not being a successful leader. Moral Leadership demands that a leader put the welfare of people first.

The key factor, then, in effective leadership is morality and moral values. The degree to which leaders adhere to moral values is the degree to which they will be successful. The ambiguity in the phrase "moral values" must be clarified. Morality and moral values is not religious in nature. Many religions use morality as an important part of their beliefs, but the term itself, and the conduct depicting morality, is not religious. A closer tie would be ethics.

Even "spiritual values" are not necessarily religious, for "spiritual" is most often contrasted with material, physical, or corporeal (rather than God or religion). In fact, *The Oxford Dictionary* defines *spiritual* as "of spirit as opposed to matter." It defines *spirit* as the "intelligent or immaterial part of man, soul." These definitions suggest the dual nature of humankind—spiritual and material. A human being functions through both the physical body and also through the intellect and will. These uses of the terms are common—attempting to separate tangible or physical activity and standards with those not physical. Morality, then, often associated with the spiritual part of man rather than the physical, refers to actions that might be seen in any human being in any country and of any religious belief whatsoever.

Therefore, even though moral standards might vary in different cultures, some basic tenets are similar—it is usually considered wrong to steal from another in any culture—thus stealing is an immoral act and a moral person would not do so. This is a philosophical or secular value—not religious. For this reason Rick Garlikov, in his article "Moral and Spiritual Values" can qualify that "Moral laws are general, sometimes abstract, principles about how things ought to be"; . . . discovered through our "collective moral sensitivity, understanding, judgment, and wisdom" (3). Moral ideas, then, are right or wrong depending on their content, what they say, rather than on who said them.

Moral reasoning leads us to apply the principles of morality to any situation or issue at any time. Leadership is no exception. And perhaps it is even more important to use all the moral sense we have when we lead, even more so than at any other time, because our followers are watching and learning from us. Let's look, in the next section, at some specifics of moral leadership.

## Moral Leadership

The very highest leader is barely known by men.

Then comes the leader they know and love.

Then the leader they fear.

Then the leader they despise.

The leader who does not trust enough will not be trusted.

When actions are performed without unnecessary speech

The people say, "We did it ourselves."

- Lao Tsu

"Leadership" is a word which implies a process that is fairly well-known. We all know what the term means—at least we think we do. And most of us would agree that we know what "moral" means—at least in an amorphous, ambiguous way we do. It is, after all, a non-tangible word, and hence the definition will vary from culture to culture, from situation to situation, even from person to person, and therefore it is not easy to define specifically. To clarify the point being made by "moral leadership," then, it is important to define and illustrate the terms in the ways intended for this book and this chapter.

Leadership is a process and a set of practices. Therefore, leadership is amoral—the processes and practices are neither right nor wrong. All processes can be used for good or evil; therefore it is the use of such process that can be associated with morality or immorality. Leaders, on the other hand, are definitely moral or immoral, though their moral or immoral actions are not as easily identified. The society under which the leader works determines whether the actions of that leader are moral or immoral. For example, James Kouzes and Barry Posner, in *Credibility: How Leaders Gain and Lose it, Why People Demand It*, acknowledge that "Charles Manson may have been an insanely skillful practitioner of the art of leadership in the amoral sense of the term, but he was not a moral leader" (66). People like Manson, who lead others into paths not approved by the society they live in, have no legitimacy as moral leaders because they violate the shared values of the societies from which they come.

The true test of moral leadership, says leadership scholar James MacGregor Burns, is when a leader's actions are "grounded in conscious choice among real alternatives. Any leader who would impose his or her will upon others and allow them no choice is not morally legitimate" (*Leadership*, 36). Leaders must decide what they stand for, and they must allow the constituencies to choose their leaders based on those stands or moral judgments that leaders stand for. And followers do want to follow those who exhibit moral leadership.

In fact, in another book by James Kouzes and Barry Posner, *The Leadership Challenge: How to Keep Getting Extraordinary Things Done in Organizations,* the authors report the results of a questionnaire they gave to several thousand business and government executives. They asked the question, "What values (personal traits or characteristics) do you look for and admire in your superiors?" Many traits were identified of course, but the surprising result was that the top four traits desired were invariably the same; executives wanted leaders to be Honest—88%, Forward-Looking—75%, Inspiring—68%, and Competent—63% (21). Notice that the top choice had to do with the moral stance of the leaders, not the ability or knowledge we might assume would be first. This kind of result would lead us to believe that whatever people say, they really want moral leadership; the moral side of a leader tends to give others a sense of security.

To create high morality in any organization or group, we must hold the right values. Historically, some of the proponents of value system leadership have taken a neutral position on values clarification. Such a position has weakened the stand leaders must take. For example, Merrill Harmin states "Our emphasis on value neutrality probably did undermine traditional morality, . . . It makes a good deal of sense to say that truthfulness is better than deception, caring is better than hurting, loyalty is better than betrayal, and sharing better than exploitation" (24-30).

Though almost everyone might agree that leaders should be honest and moral, how do we choose leaders in the first place? Are some simply born to be leaders while others are born to be followers? Leaders do not tumble out of the sky full-blown and credible. Some legitimizing process opens the door to provide leadership for us. In fact, followers often are the key to an effective leader. Someone said, "if you think you are a leader, look behind you. If anyone is following, you are a leader." Some leaders are appointed by others. Some simply emerge—no one else is leading and someone has to. Some are very reluctant to take over any kind of leadership, but will do so if coerced strongly enough by a group. Others love to lead and just automatically take over whenever there is a leadership opportunity.

Whatever the circumstances under which one becomes a leader, though, there is no question about the truth of the following statement: **who you are determines what you do as a leader.** Though many would agree offhandedly with that statement, it is the expressed opinion of James David Barber, Duke University's political scientist. Barber thinks the personalities of American presidents can be studied to predict their performance in office. Barber points out that executives are either "active" or "passive" in their actions as leaders, and they are also either "positive" or "negative" in their pursuit of power and their goals. Barber categorizes our past Presidents accordingly. He sees both Roosevelts, John Kennedy, and Harry Truman as "active-positives." They were active in their relationships and comfortable with the exercise of their offices. Tragedy-prone presidents, such as Nixon and Lyndon Johnson, are considered "active-negative" because of their negative use of power. Reagan, Harding, and Taft are "passive-positives" in Barber's view because they weren't able to exercise initiative toward others easily. Coolidge is one example of a "passive-negative" president (Barber, 367-390).

What is the point of all that? To verify that our characters will probably predict our leadership styles. We act on what we value. If we are very active and positive people, our leadership will reflect active and positive actions. If our standard of morality is high, our leadership will reflect that morality. None of us is a better leader than we are a person. Many people might seem to be a better leader than they are a person. However, think back over the past few years and note how many apparently "wonderful" leaders actually fell into immorality or disgrace or deceptive practices—all because they pretended to be more moral in the public eye than they really were. Morality is lacking when there is any violation of trust or violation of integrity or when there is any mistreatment of other human beings.

Margaret Thatcher, former Prime Minister of Great Britain, gave the concluding lecture in the Seminar at Hillsdale's Center for Constructive Alternatives. She examined how the Judeo-Christian tradition has provided the moral foundations of America and other nations in the West, and she contrasts the United States' experience with that of the former Soviet Union. She states "The Moral Foundations of the American Founding History has taught us that freedom cannot long survive unless it is based on moral foundations" (1).

America's founding years bear witness of that truth, continues Ms. Thatcher. Though the United States has become the most powerful nation, yet she uses her power not for territorial expansion but to perpetuate freedom and justice through the world. The United States believes in freedom for all men. Such a belief springs from her spiritual heritage, which began with the founding fathers. John Adams, second president of the United States, wrote, "Our Constitution was designed only for a moral and religious people. It is wholly inadequate for the government of any other" (Thatcher, 1). Former President Calvin Coolidge said that "the foundations of our society and our government rest so much on the teachings of the Bible that it would be difficult to support them if faith in these teachings would cease to be practically universal in our country" (Thomas, 4).

John Winthrop, who led the Great Migration to America in the 17th century and who helped found the Massachusetts Bay Colony, declared, "We shall be as a City upon a Hill"; he told the people that they must "learn to live as God intended men should live: in charity, love, and cooperation with one another. . . . Most of the early colonists . . . tried to live in accord with a Biblical ethic" (Thatcher 1). It took tremendous courage for American colonists to set out on a dangerous journey to fulfill their faith.

The faith of America's founders affirmed the sanctity of each individual—every human life was equal in the eyes of the Lord God. The Ten Commandments of Moses gave people a sense of obligation toward each other, observes Thatcher (2).

Pre-Christian philosophers such as Plato and Aristotle knew that responsibility was the price of freedom. Sir Edward Gibbon, author of *The Decline and Fall of the Roman Empire,* judged that in the end the Athenians wanted security more than freedom. Yet they lost everything—security, comfort, and freedom—because they wanted not to give to society but for society to give to them. The freedom they were after was freedom from responsibility (Thatcher 2). No wonder they fell. As long as freedom is grounded in responsibility and morality, it will last. Free societies are the only societies with moral foundations, and those foundations are evident in their political, economic, legal, cultural, and most importantly, spiritual lives (Thatcher 5).

In many areas Western civilization and the American way of life have risen to the highest standards of honor, justice, morality, and the esteem for life. It is obvious that these qualities are the foundation of western progress—actually have been the foundation of western life for hundreds of years. But recently the issue of the value we give to life came along to be tested. The issue is not simply abortion, but the value we give to life (Joyner 57). In nature the preservation of life is the most basic and powerful motivation. Consequently, except for a few of the lowest forms of species, family is a primary drive of life. Few creatures in existence will not quickly sacrifice their own lives to protect their young. It is unnatural for a mother to destroy her child, born or unborn; such an action reveals a fundamental departure from civilization and a moving toward fundamental barbarism. Joyner believes that there will be no peace of mind on earth until life is esteemed above ambition or convenience (58). It is not difficult to see that the preservation of life is fundamental to nature and to morality.

Just because something is legal does not make it right. Fundamental laws prevail in nature, and these laws reveal that the true nature of morality is doing what is right—regardless of mere legal compliance. A civilization that is not based on law will degenerate into despotism and tyranny. But a civilization that cannot rise above the law to live by what is moral (not just legal) has degenerated already and has lost its potential for true greatness. Just as lawlessness results in tyranny, so will the inability to rise above the law for morality's sake result in tyranny (Joyner 58).

The primary decline in the American family (and in American productivity) is selfishness. Family is primordial. History will verify that the quickest way to destroy a civilization is to destroy the morality which esteems the family (Joyner 59). After the family, people should be the greatest concern. To see an enterprise or company as a "thing" is to dehumanize the enterprise and the people who comprise it. People are never "things" to control or manipulate. The concept applies to any organization and the people who support that organization as well as to a literal family unit. The people who comprise the company are more important than the profits or the esteem of the company itself.

"The Founding Fathers' vision was for a constitutional republic where the will of the people would be imposed on Washington, not the views of Washington imposed on the people" (Ashcroft 1). In referring to the intentions of the founding fathers, John Ashcroft quotes Hamilton who declared, in his famous phrase, "Here, Sir, the people govern" (1). And Ashcroft asks, Can it still be said that the people govern the United States? (1-4).

For leadership to be successful, it is essential that one delineate the necessary qualities, characteristics, and approaches for leadership of each specific environment. Some people project the future directions of our country and world, specifying which leadership styles may be relevant for the future businesses and governments. However, forecasting techniques will always have limits; we still cannot be certain what the future will bring. Decrane, though, suggests that there is one model that can help us put some meaningful concepts into leadership in business. He calls it the "constitutional model" because James Madison and other framers of the U. S. Constitution "constructed a document embodying certain core principles to guide the lives of the American people and to establish the framework of governance" (250). These framers constructed a document that had to be worded broadly enough to be effective for many specific daily issues as well as for changing conditions and for future challenges they could not even envision. Even so many years later, in the 21st century, we still see that the fundamental principles guiding the Constitution continue to survive, regardless of the huge number of amendments and attempts to interpret them in ways amenable to specific purposes.

In the same way, core qualities of leadership can be identified, even though they may need to be qualified and modified and reapplied as conditions change and new challenges arise. The truly basic qualities remain solid and relevant (Decrane 250). Those core qualities of leadership would include, in addition to basic leadership skills, Character, Vision, Behavior, and Confidence. These traits endure despite all social, political, cultural, and business changes. These basic leadership principles help individuals at all stages of responsibility to lead and to model what a leader should be. The constitutional model suggests that leaders will adapt these core competencies to the challenges of their time and the areas of their responsibilities.

Community occurs when free people with some sense of equal worth join together voluntarily for a common goal. This is most easily done in small organizations affording face-to-face contact. Larger organizations find it difficult to create enough personal contact and common vision to guide actions down the hierarchy of leadership. The larger and more complex the organization/group, the more difficult it is to reach a common vision and derive enough community spirit to guide actions without also increasing the chain of command. The larger the chain of command, the more freedom necessary for community to become undone. As the power of community spirit is stretched thin, the chain of command fills the void, and the sense of community declines further (Pinchot, 28).

The organizations that first hit the wall of complexity and thus were in need of institutions to distribute leadership were the largest organizations of all—whole societies and nations. Leaders of successful nations, then, have become the models of good leadership techniques. Centuries ago nations began reaching the limits of direct leadership. The diversity of tasks was simply too great for any one king or dictator to run everything effectively (Pinchot, 29). Western European nations gave the free market a major role in their economy. The nations in the Warsaw Pact, who ran their economies with centrally controlled ministries, fell behind in wealth and human contentment. China, by freeing her nation's entrepreneurial spirit from the Communist party, has allowed its leaders to achieve double-digit economic growth. South Korea, Chile, Singapore, Peru, and Taiwan have all achieved economic growth after freeing their markets. Could the same level of growth in productivity and innovation become available to leaders of corporations? The more freedom allowed, the more indirect the leadership. Since direct leadership has imposed limitations, the largest groups, especially nations, must move into free enterprise and indirect leadership.

As the complexity of an organization reaches beyond direct leadership, the leader's main purpose is contributing to the corporate culture and the corporate institutions that make freedom work and that create a freer society within the organization (Pinchot, 38). The freer society will be based on values such as respect for all people, freedom of choice and speech and assembly, fairness, and justice. The leadership, at this point, will be the best kind of government of a free nation. Leaders of this kind will bring out the best in others and will listen to their followers.

Our founding fathers seem to have seen that the day would come when "liberty would hang in a balance. . . . they believed that liberty cannot survive without morality. Our liberties are in danger because Americans have become an immoral people. . . . A majority of Americans say that character isn't important in political leaders" (Mostert, note, p. 1). Calvin Coolidge, however, showed a great deal of insight when he stated that "if we are to maintain the great heritage which has been bequeathed to us, we must be like-minded as the fathers who created it. . . . . We must follow the spiritual and moral leadership which they showed" (Thomas 5). Coolidge pointed out that the foundations of our country were not material, but spiritual and moral: "no other theory is adequate to explain or comprehend the Declaration of Independence . . . it is the product of the spiritual insight of the people" (Thomas 5). And Coolidge concludes by asserting that "unless the faith of the American people . . . is to endure, the principles of our Declaration will perish" (5).

Consequently, though many today may say that character is not important in leaders, we have much evidence that character and morality are indeed as important in leadership as they are in other areas of our American way of life. In fact a big advertisement in the *Wall Street Journal*, for October 5, 2003, announcing the availability of a new book for corporate leaders (Bill George, *Authentic Leadership: Rediscovering the Secrets to*

*Creating Lasting Value*), led out with this large-type heading: "Character still counts!" And it definitely has counted for years. Calvin Coolidge stated we do not need more intellectual power, we need more moral power. We do not need more knowledge, we need more character" (Thomas 6). His statement is still true today.

## Bibliography

Dale, Robert D. *Ministers as Leaders.* Nashville, Tenn: Broadman Press, 1984.

Garlikov, Rick. In his article "Moral and Spiritual Values." Internet, pp 1-3.

Haas, Howard G. *The Leader Within: An Empowering Path of Self-Discovery.* New York: HarperBusiness, 1992.

Kouzes, James M., and Barry Z. Posner. *The Leadership Challenge: How to Keep Getting Extraordinary Things Done in Organizations.* San Francisco: Jossey Bass, 1987.

Scarborough, Joe, U. S. Representative. "Public Display of the Ten Commandments," House of Representatives Speech, March 3, 1997, printed on Internet *Must Read List.*

Ashcroft, John. "Moral Leadership in Politics (or the Judiciary?)" *Mediafax Technologies,* Inc., 1997, pp. 1-4.

Barber, James David. *The Presidential Character: Predicting Performance in the White House.* Englewood Cliffs, NJ: Prentice-Hall, 1977. Also see James D. Barber, "Adult Identity and Presidential Style: The Rhetorical Emphasis," *Philosophers and Kinds: Studies in Leadership,* ed. Dankwart A. Rustow (New York: George Braziller, 1970), pp. 367-397.

Burns, James MacGregor. *Leadership.* New York: HarperCollins, 1978.

Decrane, Alfred C., Jr. "A Constitutional Model of Leadership," *The Leader of the Future,* eds. Frances Hesselbein, Marshall Goldsmith, Richard Beckhard. Drucker Foundation Future Series. San Francisco: Jossey-Bass Pub., 1996, pp. 249-256.

Harmin, Merrill. "Value Clarity, High Morality: Let's Go for Both," *Educational Leadership* (May 1988): 24-30.

Joyner, Rick. *Leadership, Management, and the Five Essentials for Success.* Charlotte, North Carolina: MorningStar Publications, 1994.

Kouzes, James M., and Barry Z. Posner. *Credibility: How Leaders Gain and Lose it, Why People Demand it.* San Francisco: Jossey Bass, 1993.

Kouzes, James M., and Barry Z. Posner. *The Leadership Challenge: How to Keep Getting Extraordinary Things Done in Organizations.* San Francisco: Jossey Bass, 1987.

# How Should We Then Live?

## Nina May

When I was asked to speak on the value system of moderates who identify themselves as neither liberals nor conservatives, I realized that in order to understand an average, you have to define the parameters or the boundaries of that average. Likewise, in order to fully understand the concept of conservatism it has to be discussed with an understanding its antithesis, liberalism.

The irony of the term liberal is that, at first blush, it suggests liberty and personal freedom; but like its philosophy, its very name is deceptive. There have been people and movements throughout history that try to portray their struggle, movement, or governing philosophy as one that best suits the populace. The reality though, is that it can be narrowly defined as a ruling class determining for the "unwashed masses" what is best for them. This philosophy is as old as the philosophers who first defined a class structure, suggesting that only a small elite group of intellectuals and talented thinkers were capable of determining what was best for the vast majority. It was a majority whose sole purpose in life would be to make the elite more comfortable and successful so they, in turn, could better serve the masses.

This is a recurring theme in history from Plato to Marx, to W. E. B. Dubois and his theory of the "Talented Tenth." That idea was to suggest that only ten percent of the population is really gifted and talented enough to lead the other ninety percent; similarly Plato's structured, segregated and elitist society divided between the enlightened leaders and the rest who servant these leaders.

In every oppressive society you will find a similar mentality that will always suggest that a handful of gifted, enlightened people know what is best for the vast majority, whether or not this vast majority realize and embrace it, or succumb to it. Their reaction is basically irrelevant to the ruling, privileged class because to question them further illustrates that the masses truly are too ignorant to know what is best for them. This was the argument that Marx and other oppressive thinkers used to determine that the masses are too ignorant to think for themselves. They decided, unilaterally, that this communal group of people would have all the decisions made for them, because they are considered, by virtue of this philosophy, to be inferior, less enlightened, therefore unequal in every way. They were virtually a separate slave class that could be congratulated, manipulated, or annihilated at will.

This is because the very foundation of the liberal mentality is that there are no absolutes, that right and wrong are determined by the ruling class. Elitism necessarily breeds contempt for those who are ruled. In liberalism, some men has determined themselves to be god-like in nature and worthy of determining the fate of other human beings. There is no true compassion for those who fail to rise to the level of the elite, yet liberals see their role as benevolent dictator, as compassionate and empathetic because, historically, they would allow their subjects to live, occasionally rewarding them for small victories.

Today, benevolence is paraded out by liberals in the form of government handouts and class conflict that pits one group of citizens against another. The interesting thing though, is that liberal's generosity is shown with the hard earned wages of those who do not need or want government assistance. Yet their work and effort is taxed, nonetheless, to make this self-appointed, ruling class seem benevolent and compassionate.

The antithesis of liberalism is conservatism, which, unfortunately, has been mischaracterized as a restrictive, intolerant, unforgiving philosophy that tries to dictate beliefs and value systems. The irony is that this definition better fits "liberalism," for a variety of reasons. In the United States today, although the country was established on Judeo-Christian, godly principles (with these founders even suggesting that to found a country on any other principles would doom it to failure), to mention these principles or the truth of its establishment is considered intolerant. The revisionists have misinterpreted the freedom of religion in the First Amendment as being freedom *from* religion; the state should not be allowed to support even a mere discussion of religion. That is the true intolerance that has permeated our society to the point where the Bible, the Ten Commandments and any vestige of Judeo-Christian principles and beliefs have been eradicated. Yet Christians are the ones who are considered intolerant and judgmental.

The reality of conservatism is that at its core is belief in self-determination, individuality and personal liberties which are inherent to the nature and existence of man. Conservatives truly do believe that all men are created equal by their Creator, endowed with certain inalienable rights, including the right to life, liberty, the pursuit of happiness. These foster freedom from oppression by another man or woman, and the right to determine where that ultimate freedom takes them. The conservative system, at its core, has man as a creation of a higher being, God, who made man in His image to live freely among His other creations, to be fruitful, multiply and live a long and joyful life. The hope, of course, of the Creator is that man will recognize the God-shaped void in their life and seek to draw closer to Him. In conservatism, that freedom is nurtured and encouraged, whereas in liberalism, it is discouraged because there is no recognition of a higher source of power than fallen man, who ironically, denies that he is fallen.

This dichotomy or conflict is as old as man and has, as its core, original sin, juxtaposed with ultimate, eternal redemption and salvation. God has made a very simple path from and out of sin, to an eternal relationship with Himself. Yet, those who deny God also wish to deny the opportunity to discover this path to those who instinctively want to traverse it. That is the eternal conflict that continues today, but thankfully, was silenced and suppressed long enough to found this country on

Judeo-Christian principles that acknowledge man's fallen nature, yet encourage man to seek his Creator for redemption. That path is getting darker as the nation ages, while vines of doctrine and stones of cynicism make it both harder to see the path, and more difficult to inspire a desire to walk it.

Those who have been blessed to follow the path of truth that leads them to a relationship with the Creator have been derelict in their duty to keep that path clear for others to find and experience. They have allowed themselves to be caught in the trap of appearing intolerant or judgmental, forgetting that the one and only thing that separates their philosophy and belief from unbelievers is the Love of God. They have forgotten the words of Christ who implores us to love one another as we love ourselves, to love God with all our hearts. Against love there is no law.

The basic foundation of the conservative philosophy is the absolute knowledge that God ordained each of us to live freely within the confines of ten basic laws that were designed by Him to make that life happier, more peaceful, more productive and more meaningful for eternity. The first five laws in the Ten Commandments deal with our relationship to God, confirmation that indeed He is real, we are made in His image and He wants to love us intimately. He does not want us to set up idols or worship false gods, or use His name in vain, and He wants to commune with us at least one day a week to remind us of His love for us.

The second five commandments deal with our relationship to each other, but as Christ said, if you have love in your heart, and let love guide all that you do, you will, by default, be keeping all ten commandments. You will be loving God with all your heart, you will be loving your neighbor as yourself and not wanting to be envious, or covetous with any of his possessions. You will not want to kill him, cheat him, bear false witness against him, or steal his belongings, because those actions are in direct conflict with the power of love, which is the definition of God.

So, ironically when we think of sin, it is not so much that sin is an affront to God, it is the act of committing the sin that separates us from God based on the very simple law He gave us, which is to love. The reality of Hell is the knowledge of good and evil and the understanding that we will be separated from God for eternity. It is the knowledge that we will be separated from love for eternity and nothing we can do will ever fill that void except the knowledge, pain, despair and anguish of eternal separation.

The philosophy of conservatism is based on the belief that there is a higher being, that God loves us and wants to have a relationship with us and wants us to live our lives in peace with one another, determining our own destiny based on His gifting and leading. It is a philosophy based on freedom, not license, on rights, responsibilities, and on a foundation of absolutes that cannot be denied or challenged by man. To deny the existence of God is to deny that man has a purpose or a destiny, and it is to equate his existence with all other living creatures on earth. This is basically the foundation of liberalism.

In George Orwell's book, *Animal Farm*, animals are taught that they are equal to man, yet even they had a structure that determined some animals to be "more equal" than others. This is the basis of the liberal mindset, which has at its core, supremacy, elitism, privilege and position. It feigns equality for the purpose of convincing the masses that we are all the same, yet the common denominator is always that of follower, oppressed victim, or silenced protestor. Those who set the system of liberalism in place understand clearly that their position is superior and they must, in order to maintain that position, separate themselves from those they claim to represent. There is mock approachability as lords walk through crowds of bowed servants, as dictators wave at throngs of adoring subjects waving matching flags, wearing matching uniforms, sporting matching smiles for fear of appearing different, under penalty of death. Similarly, in our democracy, liberals who represent or speak for the masses do so from behind the tinted glass of limos and private jets, mansions and red carpet experiences, allowing the adoring masses to catch sight of, and breath in, their "holiness." They have set themselves up as saviors to their subjects, as objects of affection and adoration to those who have been taught by these very people that there is no God, no truth, no eternity and no reason to exist other than to give these self-appointed leaders authority to lead everyone else's lives.

Conservatives, like Jesus, are the true revolutionaries who challenge status quo, shake man's definition of the establishment, and change the paradigm of how man naturally responds to life. The natural man fulfills his own personal desires regardless of whom it might hurt or inconvenience. The conservative realizes that unless tethers and governors are put on our passions, society will not long endure. The natural man is selfish, greedy, self-absorbed and ignorant of the needs of those around him. That is, unless the natural man makes a concerted and specific effort to do as God suggests, to love his fellow man as himself. This is indeed a very difficult, and unnatural state for fallen man to be in, although it can be, and has been done. When a U. S. citizen, who selflessly chooses military service, falls in the line of duty or in combat, that person has given his life for the freedom of his fellow man. There is no greater love than for one person to give his life for another, but that again is in conflict with the natural inclination of man.

The distinction though, between a war fought to preserve freedom and one fought to destroy personal freedom, is the very nature of spiritual conflict. A conservative army (using the above definition of conservative, not the political definition) will understand as he prepares for battle, that he may never return, but his sacrifice will be one that will be remembered and honored forever, because those who were saved were given the freedom to continue to live. For armies sent to fight by liberals (based on the definition of liberal given above), it is not about preserving freedom, but oppressing those they are fighting against. The perfect example of that is World War Two when the conservative allied forces joined to stop the spread of genocide and global domination that the liberal forces of Germany and Japan were designing for the world. For the United States, involvement in that war was not as much an act of self preservation as of unselfish sacrifice of life, so that others might live, so the dying might end.

The collectivist, inhuman philosophies of communism, socialism, slavery and abortion have caused the deaths of millions upon millions of people in the world, while the hope of democracy and conservative governments, based on a foundation of absolutes, have given life to millions of people. That is why the United States stands before the world as a shining city on a hill that attracts millions and millions of people fleeing oppressive, liberal regimes, seeking peace, sanctity and hope. They are coming out of failed liberalism to a conservative country that is filled with millions and millions of people who recognize that there is a sovereign God who is intimately involved in the affairs of man.

Without a conservative philosophy, based on the absolute knowledge and mandate to follow a risen Savior sent from a loving God to show the world how we should then live, the world would be dominated, oppressed, subjugated and eventually annihilated. The ones who were not murdered, tortured, or abused to death would only live hopeless, godless lives of despair, having no clue as to their ultimate purpose in existing. We have seen this played out too often in history by too many dictators, oppressors, kings, emperors, Caesars, commissars, self-appointed leaders who rejected God and set themselves up to be a very poor and totally flawed substitute for Him.

A contemporary issue that purely reflects this conflict between conservative and liberal, right and wrong, good and evil, is the issue of abortion. Because conservatives see all life as precious, with a specific purpose and destiny designed by their Creator, they see conception as a miracle. Because liberals deny the unique existence of man as reflection of a higher being, incapable of anything more than taking up space on a crowded planet, they see the most merciful or practical thing to do is to end that life. They have proven that not only do they dismiss the existence of a higher being, they have determined themselves to be in that role, playing god with the lives of the unborn. This conflict, like the issue of slavery that divided the nation is, at its core, the conflict between right and wrong, love and hate, freedom and oppression.

We see it in many countries around the world today, and even in our country. This is not to say that all who reject the divinity of God as Creator are destined to oppress those less fortunate or be inclined to do evil deeds. The sad irony is that their self-proclaimed god, their leader, oppressor, emperor or potentate could not afford the masses the luxury of entertaining either evil thoughts or deeds. Liberals know the natural state of man is to rebel, is to question authority, is to determine themselves equal to or greater than a god. Thus liberals need to create strong, draconian measures to keep their subjects in line, giving them small rewards for adhering to a collectivist mentality. Their subjects become little more than pets who are rewarded for obeying their benevolent dictators.

Some societies and cultures have so inbred the concept of subservient behavior that class systems are established even before birth. No one can escape the destiny of the gods to be either a slave or a master, it is a birthright. But, by the one true God, all men are created equal, yet with a specific, unique, *sui generis* destiny for each free individual.

In oppressive cultures with a handful of self-proclaimed leaders, propelled by force or a cultural heritage, there is little room for opposition or rebellion. Those who comply and acquiesce to domination are told they are fulfilling a higher cause. But the moment they try to embrace that cause, or actualize it, and it conflicts with the dictates of the sovereign, they are rebuked or killed. So the most effective liberal dictator will erect false walls of security and happiness that placate their subjects and tell them they are good and are serving mankind by their submissive attitude.

Since liberals have determined that nature is to be worshipped, that the climate is fragile and must be maintained or the earth will take offense, those without a supreme God to worship will be inclined to believe it, making nature their god. Virtue then is defined by how much you sacrifice to this god, how you protect it, and to what extent you will go in proving your worth by committing your entire life to its well-being.

There are those who have replaced the worship of God with the worship of animals to the point that the human being is an offense to the existence of animals. If given a choice between a man or an animal, the animal is given priority.

Many worship power over God and will subject the masses to the lies and distortions of their reality to give the appearance of perfection. In the 2008 presidential elections there is a candidate who was being equated to a modern day savior because he manipulates and regurgitates two words repeatedly until they take on a life of their own: hope and change. The mesmerizing effect of these two words, without substance to support their meaning, gives flights of fancy to the enthralled followers who hope for change, not even knowing what they want to change.

When the one true God has been replaced by people who are arrogant in their ignorance, then they can no longer make decisions that are in the best interest of mankind because they have chosen to obey the basest characteristic of man, total satisfaction of the natural self. That separation from God is, at its core, the essence of liberalism, while the very foundation of conservatism and self-restraint is the acknowledgment that all men have sinned, and fallen short of the glory of God. Yet redemption is at hand in the person and deity of Jesus Christ who paid the ultimate price for all of us; He loved us unto death, redeemed us in resurrection and is with us today by the grace of the Holy Spirit who will, and does, guide those who ask "how should we then live?"

Nina May is the founder and chairman of Renaissance Foundation. She is a producer and director of the award-winning documentary Emancipation Revelation Revolution. Nina is married to her husband Colby and has been blessed with one son. For more information on Nina and her work visit rwnetwork.net

# Conservatives and Compassion: Equal Partners in Saving Life

## Bradley Mattes, M.B.S.

There are many critical issues facing society today. Anyone thirty-five years of age or older has witnessed a significant erosion of America's morals and values. When we compare life today with the generation of the fifties, it hardly resembles a people of the same planet.

The conservative mind mourns the passing of many things that made life righteous and good. Those who have a passion for justice and fairness, who believe in personal responsibility, individual rights and precious freedoms, are particularly grieved by the most egregious injustice of our time – the legal killing of tens of millions of innocent unborn children.

Future historians, if the world is allowed to continue that long, will be hard pressed to find cruelty on the level of what is happening in abortion mills throughout our nation. Early pro-abortion pioneers, using the battle cry of ending the practice of dangerous back-alley abortion, have succeeded in merely relocating the entrance of the killing center from the rear to the front of the building. According to the National Center for

Health Statistics, during 1972, the year prior to *Roe v. Wade,* only 39 women died from illegal abortion, a tiny fraction of what pro-abortion activists claimed. Sadly, today it isn't uncommon to read about women who die at the hands of so-called safe and legal abortionists.

Much to the shame of America, our elected leaders hardly paused as the US Supreme Court, by edict in 1973, condemned millions of innocent preborn babies to death row via suction cannulas, dismembering forceps, looped-shaped steel knives, and salt-poisoning or head-crushing techniques. In spite of what we already knew then of the beauty and wonder of unborn life, America looked the other way in the name of feminist fervor and "Pro-choice!" catcalling.

But by God's grace and mercy, abortion also brought out the good in millions of people. Its legalization motivated compassionate citizens to form local right to life chapters and statewide organizations. Crisis pregnancy centers, staffed mostly by volunteers, began to pop up. In time, national and international pro-life organizations were developed, and eventually post-abortion counseling became relatively commonplace. Yes, the blood running from the abortion chambers, combined with the collective anguish of mothers, fathers, grandparents, aunts, uncles and even siblings, has moved many hearts of this nation to stand in the gap to face down the evil of abortion.

Our most effective tool in this life-and-death struggle has been pro-life education. Beautiful images of an eight-week-old developing baby have opened the eyes of young mothers going into abortion mills and caused them to choose an alternative to abortion that both they and their babies could live with. Classroom videos, containing footage of second-trimester development compared to abortion at the same stage of pregnancy, helped to formulate life-long, rock-solid pro-life opinions of young students previously ambivalent or permissive of abortion.

The gruesome statistics of 1.2 million abortions each year, over 3,200 every day, one every 26 seconds, has gradually made an impact with those previously willing to accept the polished slogans of those promoting this modern-day holocaust. Slowly but surely, the conscience of a nation is being awakened and stirred into action.

Just as the abolitionists of long ago resolutely toiled to overcome the legality of slavery, I am confident that we too shall follow in the footsteps of those who have gone before us and ultimately relegate legal abortion to the trash heap of society where it belongs. Like the tenacious pre-civil war Americans who battled the notion that people of color were nothing more than mere chattel, modern-day pro-lifers will not rest until unborn children also receive legal personhood.

Why has abortion become so enormously controversial? How did it grow to be the defining issue of our time – impacting and often overtaking the election and appointments of everything from a school board member to the US Supreme

Court? Abortion generates unparalleled passion because it undermines a fundamental principle on which our nation was founded – the basic right to life. Without it, no other rights can be experienced or enjoyed. The child who is denied the right to live, simply because she was conceived unexpectedly, will never take her first step, climb aboard a school bus or experience the awkwardness of her teenage years. She won't date a boy, get married or have children of her own. She will never know the joy of holding her grandchild or the pain of mourning the death of a spouse. She will have been denied every freedom and experience that you and I have the privilege of knowing today. Abortion is the most flagrant and devastating violation of human rights known to man because it automatically invalidates all other rights.

Man was created with a free will. It is central to who we are. It should come as no surprise that society would chafe and rebel against that which undermines all other rights. The debate over abortion has divided husband and wife, parent and child, neighbors, coworkers and congregations. The conflict over abortion will rage until this monster is finally beat back and defeated.

At the core of this controversy is the undeniable fact that human life begins at the moment of fertilization. This is when the woman's ovum combines with the man's sperm, beginning the life journey of a unique individual that will never be repeated. This miraculous union results in a single cell that contains everything you are today. Your hair and eye color, shoe size and future genetic makeup that may result in you developing diabetes – they're already present. All that will be added from this point on is nutrition and maturation. Medically and scientifically speaking you are a unique human being and should be afforded the basic right to life given to those already born.

Still others, ignoring scientific reality, advocate *they* should determine when this segment of society is legally human and should be protected from willful death. Some claim the developing unborn child is not human until it has a soul, while others advocate the preborn baby isn't fully human until viability – the ability to independently live outside the womb. Yet others decree the occupant in the womb is not worthy of the right to life until he or she takes their first breath of air.

It's frightening to think that society might decide who should live or die based on a particular religious belief. It is also intellectually dishonest to base it on viability, which doesn't define human life but only measures man's ability to sustain it outside the womb. Further, can a newborn child independently survive outside the womb without considerable care and attention by the parents? Those who have teenagers may well ask the same question.

No, there is far too much at stake to decide the humanity and right to life of the unborn child based on individual religious or moral viewpoints. The answer to the question of when life begins must be established on sound medical fact. Innocent human life begins at fertilization and should be protected from its earliest moment until natural death. This is where we must draw a line in the sand.

Many well-intentioned people support abortion in rare situations, or what we commonly refer to as the "hard cases." These involve pregnancies resulting from assault rape and incest. Surely, they say, you wouldn't expect to force the woman to endure pregnancy and birth which was the result of such an attack.

First, it needs to be said that less than two percent of all abortions done are for assault rape or incest. A vast majority of them are performed for social or economic reasons. Those women who become pregnant under such dire circumstances need all the love and support we can muster. However, offering abortion as a solution to a resultant pregnancy would do more harm than good for various reasons.

Abortion is a traumatic experience under any circumstance. Ending the life of a human being through abortion, even when the result of a crime, would be adding a second trauma to the sexual assault. She would then have to live with the added memory of killing her baby – yes the child is also *her* flesh and blood.

If justice is to be done following a sexual assault, the perpetrator should be prosecuted to the fullest extent of the law. Punishing the child by inflicting death is misdirected justice. The baby, like the mother, is an innocent victim of this crime. He or she should not be punished for the offense of the biological father. The option of making an adoption plan may be an alternative that both the woman and her baby can life with.

Every living, breathing person has been impacted in some way by abortion. Many of those "missing in action" could easily have directly or indirectly affected our walk in life. How many people are absent who would have developed cures for diseases or discovered inventions that would have greatly improved our quality of life? Instead they were aborted and their dreams and accomplishments were washed down the drain with their tiny mutilated bodies. Would one of them have been your spouse or the soul mate of your child or grandchild? How many parents chose abortion and denied themselves a child who would have filled a void in their heart that they never even knew existed? America will never fully comprehend the toll abortion has taken on our society and its desire to be a great nation. Our country has willingly rejected these millions of blessings, many times without the slightest idea or care of what we would be missing.

In spite of this, the anguish of abortion has left an indelible mark on millions of parents who daily struggle with the pain of a past abortion decision. These tormented mothers and fathers of aborted babies weren't told what to expect in the weeks, months and years following the intended death of their baby. As one who has counseled post-abortive fathers, I have seen the devastation and hopelessness in their eyes. The self-hatred at times is overwhelming. Even after the often-arduous healing process is finished, I have witnessed the evidence of a burdened heart when memories of their lost child come to mind. Women and men are forever changed by abortion. It doesn't just make them un-pregnant. It makes them the parents of a dead baby – a title they will carry throughout their lives. These hurting souls need our compassion, love and assistance.

The abortion industry, in its zeal to collect the cash or credit card payment for their deadly services, didn't want to burden them with any reality that might have discouraged the sale of abortion. Consider that the average abortion costs about $400. Multiply this times the 1.2 million babies killed each year and you realize the abortion industry rakes in a cool half-billion dollars annually. Abortion is a cash cow for organizations like Planned Parenthood, the nation's largest chain of abortion facilities. They and others like them have a vested interest in making sure that America continues to worship at the altar of "choice."

Abortion has not only resulted in the deaths of tens of millions of preborn children, it is responsible for unleashing an expansive disrespect for human life in other areas of society. Those advocating euthanasia were emboldened by the US Supreme Court decisions legalizing abortion throughout pregnancy. Closely paralleling the argument for abortion, they advocate the "choice" to end their own lives. Pro-euthanasia activists have gotten a foothold in Oregon and have their sights set on additional states.

Cloning and embryonic stem cell research would never have been possible without the legalization of abortion. Days-old human embryos are routinely experimented on and killed for the sake of this unproven science. In spite of stunning scientific breakthroughs with adult stem cells, and zero human treatments with embryonic stem cell research, there are still researchers who refuse to relinquish their ill-fated political agenda.

The lack of legal protection for innocent human life in its earliest days has also paved the way for in vitro fertilization, which regularly kills human embryos that appear less than desirable. Remaining or leftover embryos are commonly discarded like yesterday's newspaper. Fertility enhancement that respects all human life it creates is a rarity.

Even in the face of this slippery slope of death, I am optimistic our nation will end the wanton slaughter of the innocents. Polling shows the next generation is much more pro-life than their parents. One such study was done by UC Berkeley's Survey Research Center. Berkeley is a bastion of liberal, pro-abortion thinking, but the results showed the nation's youth aged 15-22 were noticeably more pro-life than those 27-59.

Zogby International, a highly respected polling firm, found a considerable increase in the number of young adults aged 18-29 who support a total ban on abortion. An extensive study of American college freshmen also concluded pro-life sentiment was gaining ground among this segment of the student body. A *New York Times/CBS News* poll resulted in similar findings.

One of the reasons given for the next generation's pro-life convictions is the "survivor syndrome." These kids fortunately survived their nine-month pregnancy and were not legally aborted. Kelly, a junior at Boston College, said, "When I talk about being a survivor of abortion, I am talking about it from a personal place."

If America hopes to claim its rightful place as the best nation in the world – a shining city on a hill – it must restore protection to its most tiny and defenseless citizens. My heart burns with optimism that we will right this terrible wrong, and that abortion will be diminished, like slavery, to a tragic and shameful part of our history – never forgotten but never repeated.

---

Mr. Mattes (pronounced Ma-tis) is the Executive Director and co-founder of Life Issues Institute, internationally headquartered in Cincinnati, Ohio. The organization was established to serve the educational needs of the pro-life movement. Its primary objective is to develop and disseminate, globally, effective pro-life educational material.

He is the host of, a daily radio commentary on abortion and related issues, which is carried on nearly 600 radio stations across the nation. Mr. Mattes has hosted various half-hour radio programs on topics including: the anniversary of Roe v. Wade, adoption, men and abortion, and US Supreme Court vacancies.

He also hosts a new weekly, pro-life TV program called , which is available to over 100 million households across America and throughout Canada.

Mr. Mattes is a frequent international speaker and lecturer on abortion and euthanasia, and works with other countries to establish a pro-life educational and counseling presence.

He has done considerable anecdotal research on the effects of abortion on men, and his writings on this topic have been printed in American and international publications. He has a Master's degree in Biblical Studies and Biblical Counseling. Mr. Mattes is an adjunct professor at Master's International School of Divinity where he has written and teaches a course on men and abortion.

Mr. Mattes is a veteran of the pro-life cause, with over 33 years of educational, political and humanitarian experience. Currently, he serves in a variety of ways to protect innocent human life:

A men's post-abortion counselor.

Media spokesperson with television, radio and newspaper.

Speaker at pro-life banquet and educational events.

He resides in the greater Cincinnati area with his wife. They have four sons and two grandchildren.

# Larger than Life

## D. Wilson Nance, Ph.D.

The conservative mind matters simply because the conservative understands that life is larger than life. There's more to our lives than meets the eye.

I have a couple of friends who happen to be physicians. They tell me they frequently find themselves forced to address a patient's symptoms, such as a headache or a rash. But, they aren't satisfied with focusing on the symptoms. So, research physicians continually hunt the transcendent or fundamental cause of the obvious problem.

This leads me to my point: the conservative mind matters in an America with very real and seemingly insolvable problems. The conservative mind pays attention and gives serious thought the transcendent issues behind our struggles. And these foundational ideas are the foundation for our hopes, our ambitions and solutions.

I will explore three fundamental ideas our founders constantly had in their minds as they created our national system. Conservatives are deeply skeptical of any solution that is merely a pain pill masking the real problem. These ideas may seem a bit mysterious, and even mystical, but they are the very essence of any solution for our America.

## The Conservative Mind Remembers the Symbol of Columbia

I sometimes enjoy late-night television man-on-the-street interviews about important historical facts. But I've seen these too many times to be amazed at how few people know important ideas. Take for instance, what the D. C. of Washington, D. C. stands for. Most apparently don't know that it stands for District of Columbia. But what if the television host asked them "what is Columbia?" They might identify it as the name of a space shuttle. But I suppose, other than "I don't know," the usual answer would be Christopher Columbus.

Yet, why would our founders be keen on honoring him? I don't doubt that our framers were more aware of Christopher's importance than modern graduates. Yet, I also know they were more concerned with honoring ideas than with honoring a man.

Columbia: think of the image or statue so often associated with monuments, buildings and symbols of the American revolution and government. Most of us are familiar with a robed female, blinded with a cloth, holding balance scales. This is the goddess, or lady Justice and is a symbol of justice in the courts.

But aside from our courtrooms, we often see another robed female figure. She usually has a cap or soft hat (often in her hand) and a short stick. In recent times she is more commonly known as "Lady Liberty" (since we don't like goddesses). But in fact, she is a depiction of the goddess Columbia. From ancient Roman times the cap and pole she carries were associated with the freedom of slaves, redemption of the oppressed and opportunity for the hopeless.

But, our founders knew that Columbia was not actually a Greek or Roman goddess. Rather, she gradually took shape in political writing in the years before our revolution. Therefore she was well known to our founders. Being aptly named, "children of the enlightenment," they used this symbol.

This is what the D.C. stands for. Our capitol is to be a city of freedom for the oppressed, where tyrants are checked and liberty is exercised with responsibility, offering everyone opportunity. It was envisioned as a district where the idea of Columbia – responsible, redemptive freedom – reigned.

So how does the idea of responsible, redemptive freedom apply to modern problems? Why is Columbia relevant?

## The Conservative Mind Values the Conservation of Power

Many genuinely patriotic thinkers suggest that we ought to grant the government the power to solve our problems. But Columbia recognizes that a government's power comes from only one place: the people. And, like money, there is only so much power to be distributed. Also like money, once in someone's hand, it is seldom released back to its original owner.

When the people give up their power to the government, that power no longer exists in the hands of the people, regardless of political speeches to the contrary. It is in the hands of bureaucrats (even politicians can't usually hold the power we grant them). And, unfortunately, short of revolution, power once granted to bureaucrats is seldom ever returned.

This has ramifications for the debate on taxes which fuel governmental power. It influences welfare, health care and even wage policies. These are, at heart, nothing other than grants to our government of the power to transfer our wealth from one individual to another.

And, maybe we might want to force some redistribution. After all, health care and education are sticky issues. But, I am saying that we need to understand that every such decision needs to be considered in light of the reason our revolution happened: Columbia – neither confiscation, corruption nor coercion (all of which exist in a powerful bureaucratic government). If we give money to the government for schools, they will not give it back to us to try another way, even when their way fails miserably. If we give money to the government to provide health care, they will never give it back no matter how inept the system becomes. To ignore this in these debates is foolish.

## The Conservative Mind Values the Concept of Redemption

The redemptive aspect of Columbia is crucial to what our founders achieved. Columbia became closely associated with the New World, in the mind of the Europeans. They chafed under many limits, imposed by governments, religions and cultures. But when these varied peoples came to the New World they couldn't merely rejoice in their release.

They needed to rein in their desire to repay their old oppressors for centuries of oppression. Tit-for-tat would bring the old destruction to the New World. For, in fact, America was populated by many different groups, all of which had been involved in centuries of fighting among themselves. Germans had fought French who had fought English, who had fought Scots who had fought Irish who...on and on. But don't forget the Germans who had fought Germans, French who had fought French, English who had... again, on and on. And Catholic versus Protestant versus Puritans, versus....

What the New World settlers needed was a new start, not just for themselves but for their neighbors. So, in large measure they adopted, out of necessity, a forgive and forget approach.

Well, maybe not forget. But forgive and get along. Each needed to rely on his neighbors' strengths. Neighbors needed to trust each other; their lives were constantly at risk. The Revolutionary War succeeded largely because our ancestors overlooked the many Old World squabbles among themselves. As the current phrase goes, they covered each other's back. They achieved the dream of Columbia only because they were willing to replace vengeance with redemption.

The transcendent or foundational idea of redemption is simply this: take the sins and faults that exist and turn them to advantage. Turn weaknesses into strengths. Change rupture into relationship, creating a strong social fabric woven of cloths with

differing characteristics. Each contributes its strength while having its weaknesses reinforced.

Redemption is, of course, biblical. And the Bible was ever-
present in the education of those who began the American experiment. One example of redemption is the way the early
founders fought elections, but then put aside their battles.

They were vicious. A modern student who read what John
Adams (second President) and Thomas Jefferson (second Vice-
President, third President) said about each other, might wonder
how anyone on either side, could govern in cooperation with
people they had so savagely insulted. But they did.

They understood the biblical concept of redemption, and
it was an overriding or transcendental characteristic of the decisions they took, individually and as political leaders. Yet, I don't
want to suggest that all was rosy. It was not. If the duel in which
Aaron Burr killed Alexander Hamilton is any indication, they
had animosity as great or greater than exists today.

So how does redemption relate to our situations? The conservative mind knows that fierce disagreement does not mean
the destruction of the political process. Truth, even fiercely expressed, doesn't hamper solutions. Blunt truth does not create
the hopelessness that leads some to quit and others to become
radical. Quite the opposite. Illuminated with redemption, we
can persuade those who oppose us; we can approach solutions
that disenfranchise no one.

This is true, especially in our moral debates. The debate on abortion, in fact, is a potent example of redemption. Many of our most powerful advocates for life, have themselves crushed the innocent fruit of their own wombs. Yet, they are redeeming their sin by powerfully testifying to the truth of love and hope.

They hold the door open, imploring men and women who support a culture of death to come home. Redemption closes the door on no one. Redemption removes judgmentalism. Redemption is behind the inner hope that the conservative mind offers the world. Vengeance and vendetta are far from any mind inspired by redemption.

## The Conservative Mind Values the Concept of Responsibility

The Columbia project didn't only involve the easy-to-celebrate ideas of freedom and redemption. It was laced with a heavy dose of responsibility. Without responsibility, Columbia's freedom and redemption would have had no more power over our history than cheerleaders over a scoreboard.

Responsibility, to them, didn't mean standing in front of reporters muttering a greasy *mea culpa*: "I did it. I have no excuse. I'm sorry. So let's get back to the people's business."

Our children are unfortunate to grow up with that shallow pattern as an adult definition of responsibility.

Responsibility is better defined by the words of the apostle Paul: "Do not be deceived, God cannot be used. Whatever a man plants, that is exactly what he shall harvest." There is no free lunch. Someone must pay the piper. Money doesn't grow on trees.

Our founders understood that they would impact generations. I am sure that they did not understand the full legacy of their work. Yet, I am sure they did their work with their heirs in mind. One particular example: slavery.

The founders put together a constitution that counted slaves as three fifths of one person for representation in Congress (not that the slaves were represented, of course). Abolitionists did this grudgingly, but knowingly. Many of them adamantly opposed slavery, while others preferred that the institution die of slow decline. Southern slave holders rejoiced that they would have more representation in Congress; their opponents knew that this was a beginning toward the end. They had enshrined in our founding document the fact that a slave was not merely a beast and was more than chattel property.

Of course, they were also aware of another fact: they had dropped this thick problem on their children. True, had they known just how heavy it would fall on their grandchildren, they might have tried harder. But they did try. And they did make progress. And they did not deceive themselves or their supporters by claiming victory when they had merely forged the sword. They were responsible.

One of the lies demagogue (from the Greek term for "people-leader") politicians spew, is that under their new ideas a new day will dawn with old problems solved and ancient ineq-uities set right. But responsible leaders tells us that we can be-gin. Others must finish. Inequities will always exist. We can make some things better, but paradise is actually Utopia (Latin for "no-where").

So how does the Columbian idea of responsibility touch us? Our rights do not release our duties. As Thomas Jefferson noted, a person "...has no natural right in opposition to his social duties." But further, our rights do not relieve our children of the consequences from our choices. We are responsible for any results of our policies and decisions.

Solutions we impose weigh on many lives, now and next. Politicians have left us inner cities rife with abandoned chil-dren, by welfare policies that encouraged single motherhood. As adults they don't know how to live in peace. They angrily blame every problem on their own victimhood, destroying in anger whatever they can reach.

The conservative mind knows that when we give govern-ment power, the government will lord it over our children. The conservative mind knows that when we destroy our children, whether in schools where success is measured by adolescent peers, or in the womb with surgical sterility, we shackle our grandchil-dren to lawless citizens who will be even more gullible before their "people-leaders" than our own generation.

## The Conservative Mind Values The Essentiality Of God

Conservatives are as divided as any group on the nature of God. And a few who advocate conservative policies do not believe in God. While no one would worship Columbia, a coherent conservatism depends on an integrated understanding of life.

This integrity exists in knowing that the conservative mind matters. And, the liberal mind matters. And every human life matters. Each of us is paragraph in a story much larger than himself.

The bare truth is this: without a strong concept of God then responsibility degenerates into mere blame, redemption atrophies into mere convenience and Columbia transforms into merely another opiate that elites foist on our masses: all to keep them happily paying taxes.

Freedom exists because God created us to be free. Freedom is inalienable only in that fact. Any tyrant can alienate our freedom with enough gunpowder, but he has no right to. And it is right to work for the freedom envisioned in the idea of Columbia.

Redemption exists because God turns the most hard hearted selfish rebellion into the unintended: service for those whom it abused. Any tyrant can turn people to himself if he persuades them that it is in their own best interest. Or, he can secure cooperation by assuring mutual destruction. But all such going-along-to-get-along is still selfish and self-serving. The only redemption with staying power is based on forgiveness and co-operation simply because redemption is godly.

Responsibility too, exists only in the concept of God, primarily since responsibility is nothing if not love. Not self-love. Other love.

I can remember that I was responsible for my brother and sister. I also remember thinking that responsibility meant I would come to harm, if I let harm come to them (and that was true). But I was being led to genuine responsibility, teaching me genuine love. Now I would no more act irresponsibly toward my siblings than I would bite my tongue – never knowingly. I love them. Therefore I am responsible.

But Columbian love is still more broad. I must love my neighbors, distant both in miles and time. Yet without God there is little reason to embrace either national or generational responsibility. "People-leaders" appeal to the selfishness that we are all subject to. And selfishness leaves little room for responsibility.

Responsibility, redemption and freedom. All these transcendent ideas, and others which I can't consider here, shape the conservative mind.

The conservative mind matters precisely because it is responsive to the higher and transcendent reality in which God has placed us. Today's problems are not really the problem. They are the symptoms of our inadequate response to the guiding principles our forefathers remembered.

When we disregard the deep principles, our ignorance deepens. Ignorance feeds our desperation. Desperation accelerates acceptance of shallow sound-byte speeches by people-leaders. And our problems become ever more entrenched.

The conservative mind matters: it thinks about the transcendent and foundational ideas that provide the only true hope we have for solving the problems of our time.

Dr. Nance is a writer, editor and ghost writer whose life is focused on building and raising support for a series of Christian children's homes in India.

# What is a Conservative?

## Dean Nelson

I was likely born a conservative: I am a typical oldest child who plays by the rules, seeks peace, and rocks the boat only when necessary. The irony, of course, is that a conservative today seems like a radical; what we are typically trying to conserve was jettisoned largely two generations ago. Nonetheless, its roots and seeds still exist, even if the plant is badly damaged. Here are my thoughts on what it means to be a conservative: in my case a Christian, American, black conservative.

## Respect for Tradition

I believe one of the most important aspects of conservatism is its respect for tradition. Too many adults of my generation have prolonged our adolescence, still thinking that we know it all and our parents are "out of it." A respect for tradition simply recognizes that one cannot, in a few mere decades on the planet, know more than the accumulated wisdom of one's forefathers. Just because they could not explain how a virus gains the upper hand when your immune system is compromised does not mean it is a good idea to go outside in the winter with wet hair.

This respect mitigates our youthful hubris by reminding us that we did not get where we are on our own. It whispers that our prosperous society makes all our philosophical musing possible. It helps us soberly conclude that any attempt to discard the value system that gave birth to that society will likely be hypocritical or at least self-contradictory.

I am not saying by any means that there are not cultural habits that need to be reexamined. My wife and I have elected to homeschool our children, something that is certainly out of step with the conventions of the last few decades. We just believe that any such departure should be made cautiously. As C.S. Lewis observed,

There is a difference between a real moral advance and mere innovation…It is the difference between a man who says to us: "you like your vegetables moderately fresh; why not grow your own and have them perfectly fresh?" and that man who says, "Throw away that loaf [of bread] and try eating bricks and centipedes instead."

I have grown up in the wake of the Baby Boomers who "innovated" us out of the two-parent home, the core-curriculum, and the disciplined pleasant child. They told us that the vision of heaven as a place of abundance and joy was just grand except for that pesky God who insisted on hanging around. Get rid of Him (or call everything God until His name has no meaning) and the real Utopia was just around the corner.

That is why conservatives like me are trying to reach back a little further, behind our immediate ancestors and reclaim a heritage that, for me, goes back to the days of slavery. It was a day when slaves got married secretly (because they were often forbidden to do so publicly) and used every means at their disposal to keep their families together. It was a time when black children were actually more likely to be raised by both parents then they are today. And it was an era when slaves cried out to the God of Abraham, Isaac and Jacob, not Mother Government, for their deliverance and salvation.

Of course I thank God everyday that I was raised by two wonderful parents who declined to "innovate." They had a loving marriage that ended only when the Lord called my mother home. They spanked my sisters and me when we deserved it. My father and mother worked full time, but we went to my grandma's after school. We ate dinner together around the table every night, and breakfast together most mornings. Although they grew up in the segregated South, my parents never spoke a negative word about white people nor offered any excuses for not working hard or treating people with respect. That is a tradition to build on, not discard.

## Pitiful Pitiful Man

I believe another central assumption of conservatism is the flawed nature of mankind. In short, people are pitiful.

"For I have the desire to do what is good, but I cannot carry it out. For what I do is not the good I want to do; no, the evil I do not want to do—this I keep on doing."

This pitiful nature means that humans simply cannot handle more than a certain amount of power over others without going crazy.

Thomas Sowell explained the two major views on human nature in *A Conflict of Visions: Ideological Origins of Political Struggles*. To a conservative, (what Sowell calls the "constrained" vision), man is morally limited and egocentric. His intentions and sensitivities are by themselves pointless and unproductive. The fact that he really *wants* to save the whales, or the environment or the poor has nothing to do with whether or not he has the capacity to do so. The fact that he felt just *terrible* when that most recent natural disaster took the lives of thousands did not help a soul.

This understanding of man's limited capabilities means that our best hope for good behavior is our devotion to a transcendent set of principles. These values would include all those yucky unfashionable words like duty, chivalry, loyalty, patriotism, filial piety and so on. These moral incentives offer a payout for good behavior – a good reputation, civic pride – and a penalty for bad behavior – shame and disgrace on you and yours. This might not seem the idealistic way to keep people from stealing, killing and raping, but I am not the first to observe that the police arrive at crime scenes, not "about-to-be-crime scenes" and that shame is a great deal cheaper than jail.

Sowell contrasts this understanding of human nature with what he terms the "unconstrained vision" which holds that "the essence of virtue is good intentions." These good intentions, adherents believe, lead to human happiness. So the important thing is that you really *care* about the spread of AIDS, the plight of the inner city or the number of feral cats that need to be spayed. Caring makes you a better person, and a world full of better people is a better place. Nevermind the fact that people who *care* can be compassionately incompetent.

Black people have disproportionately been on the receiving end of society's compassionate incompetence. We have been "blessed" with integrated schools that taught us moral relativism but not how to read, welfare that paid mothers not to marry the fathers of their children, and legal abortion which means that there are now fourteen million fewer of us. But it's the thought that counts, right?

## In the Immortal Words of Frederick Douglass

Everybody has asked the question... "What shall we do with the Negro?" I have had but one answer from the beginning. Do nothing with us! Your doing with us has already played the mischief with us. Do nothing with us! If the apples will not remain on the tree of their own strength, if they are worm-eaten at the core, if they are early ripe and disposed to fall, let them fall! I am not for tying or fastening them on the tree in any way, except by nature's plan, and if they will not stay there, let them fall. And if the Negro cannot stand on his own legs, let him fall also. All I ask is, give him a chance to stand on his own legs! Let him alone!

I am, by nature, a very optimistic and trusting person. I tend to give individuals the benefit of the doubt, until they prove me wrong (several times, my wife would say). I have learned, however, a healthy skepticism of mankind's ability in general. We are wired to look out for our own interests. That is not necessarily all bad: we ought to take care of ourselves. Yet, that does not mean we do not need special advice at times: a doctor, a lawyer, an accountant, and so on.

What we do not need, I have concluded as a conservative, is a fleet of supposedly superior beings flying around in private jets to tell us not to drive our cars. We do not need teachers explaining "healthy" sexual behavior to our children instead of their math facts or our government paying farmers to neither grow crops nor find a new way to make a living. What we need most often, I've concluded, is to be left alone.

## Life is Not Fair

I believe a conservative is someone who does not make excuses for himself or for those about whom he cares. Sensible parents teach their children the timeless lesson that "life isn't fair." If it were, I would not have been born in the wealthiest democracy in the world. Those Americans who fail to learn that not only is life unfair, but it is decidedly unfair in *our favor*, carry a sense of grievance over anything that does not go their way.

If my parents had tolerated whining in our house, I might have used the fact that my guidance counselor advised me to apply to vocational schools as an excuse not to achieve academically. Instead I went to Howard University and then transferred to and graduated from the University of Virginia. While at UVA, I experienced the pain of expending far more effort on my work than I had done in high school or at Howard. That pain might have been avoided if I had gone to a more rigorous high school. But at no time did it ever occur to me to ask for special treatment. I rose to the demands of my professors, albeit without wowing anyone with my GPA, and I am a better man for it.

A conservative understands that government cannot give people freedom *and* an equal life experience anymore than a school can give students an education *and* equal GPAs. A totalitarian regime, of course, could provide everyone with an equal standard of living (oppressed) and a standard-free school could give everyone straight A's (which seems to be where our schools are heading). Conservatives are willing to trade some inequality for some freedom, because we recognize that it is the best deal anyone is going to get this side of heaven.

As a conservative, I believe that freedom only works with responsibility. If people are free to basically do what they want, then they have to be responsible when they don't make the most of their options. The role of government in all this, according to the Declaration of Independence, is to secure the rights of life, liberty, and the *pursuit* of happiness. According to the preamble to the Constitution, it is to *promote* the general welfare.

So the government is supposed to safe guard my basic right to life and freedom, so that I can be free to pursue my best interests.

Now I recognize that many deep thinkers protest at this point to say that someone without enough to eat has no "freedom," and that other victims of historic injustices or tragedies failed to have their general welfare promoted. I chime back in with a deeply sympathetic refrain: "yes, because life is not fair." Once the law sees us as equals, we had better be very careful what else we ask for. As a conservative, I am hugely skeptical of human attempts to make life "fair," most specifically when they involve government power. Many sensible people have observed that the government that gives you everything can take it all away. The hungry need to be fed, the disadvantaged need to be helped, but not primarily by the federal government.

That does not mean we do not think that it is regrettable that some people have advantages over others. I wish my high school had prepared me better for college, but that did not prevent me from making the best of my opportunities. I wish more parents read imaginative literature to their children rather than parking them in front of the television, or invested more in the development of their minds than of their wardrobes. But that is their choice, not mine or anyone else's. Any government interference with the child-rearing process (outside of jailing people for criminal abuse) can only lead to very bad things.

As a conservative who accepts the fact that mankind is selfish and that life is not fair, I believe that a free market economy does not encourage greed anymore than free air encourages breathing. A free market *copes* with the reality of human nature and harnesses it for productivity. I am distinct from hard core libertarians, however. I believe that the voluntary moral self-restraint of the individual and the moral standards of a society are vital to the health of a free economy. As I mentioned earlier, shame (over cheating and stealing, for example) is far cheaper than jail, and vastly preferable to shamelessness.

## Sacred Family

Finally, as conservative, I believe that the nuclear family – husband, wife and children – has not just utilitarian value but worth that transcends the earthly realm. In an age of exponential growth in technology, I find the greatest joys in the oldest things: in God and in the wife and children He gave me. A conservative wants to conserve the traditional family because it is inherently valuable: he understands that no innovation will replace this timeless treasure, just as no diamond could out-sparkle his daughter's smile or his son's laugh.

Common sense and an honest reading of history indicate that the traditional family arrangement produces the healthiest and most stable society. Yet it is so much more. What better balm for the seemingly hopeless flaws of a man than a wife who patiently loves him through them? Is there a superior cure for the selfish nature or the smart mouth than the age-old rod of correction? My answer to both questions is, I have not found one.

As conservative, I do not have to taste every brick and centipede to confirm it is not superior to the loaf of bread I already have. If improvements can be made to the recipe, I am happy to entertain them. But I do so with a healthy skepticism to temper optimism, and a reverence for the Original.

Dean Nelson is a graduate of the University of Virginia, and has worked fulltime for Wellington Boone Ministries since 1990. He has been a campus minister for over fifteen years, and is currently the acting President of Global Outreach Campus Ministries. He has also assisted with church plants in both Virginia and Georgia.

While living in Georgia with his family for eight years, Dean began to get involved with local politics as a volunteer. He was also honored to graduate from the Coverdell Leadership Institute which trains Republicans for local and state government service and activism, as well as the United Way VIP board training program. During this time it became obvious that black Christians must receive greater training in biblical world-view if they were to take their place in the restoration of American culture.

Bishop Boone recently appointed Dean to serve as the Executive Director of the Network of Politically Active Christians (NPAC), the political education and advocacy arm of Wellington Boone Ministries. Dean and his wife, Julia, reside in Gaithersburg, Maryland and have three homeschooled children, Michaela, Amani and Brandon.

# The DNA of the Conservative Mind

## By William Owens, Jr.

The conservative mind is a reflection of a deep embedded witness of God's DNA within man as a created being. It is a reflection of the independent choices that are made on a daily basis for our families, communities and nation. It reveals both the natural inclinations of good that flow through all of creation, and the living fruit from the seed of conservative philosophy. These follow the divine design by which life ie easily grasped.

The conservative mind is not, as many would think, a movement of a select group of people. Conservatism does not mean reserved, moral, cautious or anti-liberal. Conservatism is not, as many would assume, a step away from the masses into a retreat of life apart from reality. Sure it might carry some of these ideas, but the deeper more broader idea of conservatism, to me, is living life in the most progressive and liberating expression possible. It is life without apology, life without care (not neglect) and life filled with love that works a contagious hope. It inspires, encourages and enables a self propelled celebration with those whom it touches. All of this is experienced without coercion from men.

This DNA of the conservative mind has its own power plant. It needs no rally from oceans of people or a false high from materialism, mind altering stimulants or any external created element. The DNA of the conservative mind finds its power or endowment in its very core design: GOD. He has "endowed" us with equality, and certain inalienable rights that bear witness to the design and function of this DNA.

"We hold these truths to be self-evident, that all men are created equal, that they are endowed by their Creator with certain inalienable rights, that among these are life, liberty and the pursuit of happiness." --Delaration of Independence, 1776

As we strive towards expressing the conservative mind to our family, neighbors and fellow Americans, may we do so from the core of our DNA by bearing fruit that testifies of the life that God has given, the liberty that accompanies it, and the happiness that flows from it. By doing so, their DNA will bear witness that the conservative mind really does matter.

---

William Owens, Jr. is an accomplished author of over eight books focusing on Christian maturity. He has recently started a line of writings that also include political observations from a Black American perspective . He is president and founder of Higher Standard Enterprises, Inc., a multimedia company focusing on publishing books and developing productions that speak to the issues of country and community. He is cofounder of Black Americans For Real Change along with Dr. Alveda King (www.blackarc.org). Owens has been featured on radio shows throughout the country regarding numerous issues within the scope of politics and religion. Owens and his wife, Selena, have been married for twenty-three years. They are the proud parents of four children and reside in North Carolina.

# Why the Conservative Mind Matters

## Tony Perkins and Chuck Donovan

"We are the rock that we have been waiting for."

What if a strong-minded public figure were to offer this sentiment as a slogan for his candidacy? How would his or her audience react?

If the audience were Christian, it might be struck by the use of an image associated with Peter and the founding of the church of Jesus Christ. If the audience were just a cross-section of the public, its inferences might be merely metaphorical. The speaker might just be presenting himself as a model of stability amidst a tide of change. Perhaps the slogan would be taken as a response to the relativism of the day, where one set of moral principles is regarded as no better or worse than another.

Whatever its appeal as a rallying cry, the slogan is not one we are likely to hear these days. It is, however, a theme that betokens the conservative mind, which is, above all, a disposition to find the things that matter, put them in right relation to each other, and cling to them, not out of bitterness or frustration, but out of a sense that *a public life lived without bedrock principles* is like the seed that falls on hard ground in Luke 8:6, which withers away as soon as it springs up because it lacks access to moisture.

This rootlessness is the chief danger that a conservative mind is husbanded to avoid. That mind's roots are deep and they constantly seek the light of revelation and the moisture of experience. Some of that moisture is the residue of the tears shed at the human suffering inflicted by blind Utopian ideas. Marxism and Communism represent a Utopia of radical egalitarianism that held sway over much of the world throughout the 20th century. It was not that this radical idea failed. No, it succeeded it what it wished to do, which was to crush any notion of an alternative – be that alternative God, a representative form of government, or the concept of an eternal soul.

The wages of sin are death, and Communism inflicted the maximum in the form of millions of people killed simply because they desired freedom. Nazism embodied the Utopian ideal of the nation as God and the Fuhrer as its embodiment. In his novel *The Black Obelisk* about the interwar years in Germany, Erich Maria Remarque penned the words that are sometimes misattributed to Josef Stalin, "The death of one man is a tragedy; the death of millions is a statistic." The withering away of these manmade Utopias was drenched in the blood of their victims and the tears of their families.

The conservative mind remembers the lessons of these and other tragedies, but it is most characterized by its ability to sense their approach and refuse to succumb to them. What are the principles that distinguish and form such a mind?

*The sense that what matters most precedes the existence and claims of human government.* The conservative mind knows that certain realities – God's creation, the land we live on, the air we breathe – came into being before the structures of society and the instruments of bureaucracy were formed. God's commands regarding this reality, that we "fill the Earth and subdue it" (Genesis 1:28) and, after the Fall, that "you shall eat the herb of the field, in the sweat of your face you shall eat bread" (Genesis 3: 18-19), are enjoined upon the most basic human community, that is, man and woman. The first task of living is therefore to exercise self-government and not to rule over others.

*Our rights come from the hand of God and they are, as a consequence of that and that alone, unalienable.* The founders of the United States proclaimed this insight in the Declaration of Independence. They proclaimed it but did not prove it, because it was and is an article of faith. To underscore this fact, they wrote that they held this truth to be "self-evident": that "all men are created equal, "that they are endowed by their Creator with certain unalienable rights" and that these rights include "life, liberty, and the pursuit of happiness."

About to embark on a perilous voyage to disentanglement from Great Britain, the founders knew they had need of an anchor. Their appeal to divine Providence was not a throwaway line, a vestige of religious feeling to appeal to a religious people who had come to the colonies seeking a guarantee of the right to worship as they pleased. The appeal was to something deeper. The founders knew that for our rights to be real, and not subject to the grants or retrenchments of a distant king, they must issue from the hand of God himself. No government could alter those rights or abolish them, and any government that sought to do so was itself subject to the right of the people to "alter or abolish it."

The conservative mind is deeply conscious of this fact of our creation (God's role as the author of our rights) and our nation's founding (a cause dedicated to that understanding). This consciousness is not unique to the American experience and, as we know all too well from the history of slavery, our nation's deeds did not always measures up to its foundational words. But the consciousness of the truth of God as the origin and end, the alpha and omega, of true freedom causes the conservative mind to routinely assess and reassess what government must do to move closer to that truth.

*A government of limited powers that respects institutions prior to it, such as the family, marriage, and property, cannot endure where religious conviction is absent.* On this point, the founders and every great American leader since, from Washington to Jefferson to Dr. King to Reagan, has been absolutely clear. Political parties have risen and faltered, government's reach has ebbed and flowed, but this maxim has been daily reaffirmed and reestablished in the habits of the people.

John Adams said of the U.S. Constitution, a seemingly businesslike document laying out the checks and balances among the three branches of our national government, that our nation's survival depended on religious insight. "Our Constitution was made for a religious and moral people; it is altogether inadequate for the government of any other," Adams wrote. His meaning was straightforward: what he and his fellow patriots had framed was a platform for limited government that would secure the liberty of the people. To maintain this liberty – "a Republic, if you can keep it," in Franklin's famous phrase – the people would have to govern their own impulses, to keep passions of avarice, lust and pride in check that would make communities ungovernable or require the imposition of a police state to preserve order.

Today we are seeing how rapidly the scope of government expands as family ties dissolve and basic functions, once met by parents, churches and private associations, are increasingly being transferred to government or nationalized altogether. Local and religious institutions took the lead and built schools, hospitals and treatment centers, provided cash assistance (alms) and shelter to the needy, established homes for unwed mothers, and trained workers. That has changed and the weakening of the family is a principal explanation (and further consequence). In 2006 the percentage of newborns born out of wedlock soared to 38.5 percent, a figure unparalleled in American history.

Under this dissolution in the most intimate community of all, the family, the pressure on government to grow as provider and caretaker may prove irresistible, as it has in European societies that have seen family break-up and government build-up accelerate in tandem.

*The fight for faith, family and freedom must be won if we are to preserve the nation's soul.* In late 2003, in *Goodridge v. Department of Public Health,* the Supreme Court of Massachusetts held that the constitution of the Bay State required recognition of "marriages" contracted between homosexual couples. This avant-garde notion, which the Massachusetts legislature would not have adopted of its own accord, had no basis in the state's fundamental law.

The Massachusetts constitution is the oldest written governing document in continuous use in the world. With John Adams as its primary architect, it was ratified in 1780, nearly a decade before the U.S. Constitution. Its provisions and structure make clear that its authors and ratifiers intended a sharp distinction between the legislative power, with "its equitable mode of making laws," and the judicial power, which was to deliver "impartial interpretation" of those laws. This distinction was not some kind of artifice or abstraction, but the work of conservative minds that saw it was imperative to ensure that those who make our laws are subject to the election (and therefore the power to change) of the people.

Put another way, the power to change our government officials at every level, to hold them accountable, not to be subject to the whims of unelected judges who seize the power to make laws – this power is our "rock." Any change that dilutes this power fractures both the rock of our Republic and the accountable change that is the essence of ordered liberty.

The *Goodridge* decision was poisonous as to both its result (same-sex marriage as state policy) and its mechanism (imposition by unelected judges). The distance between the constitution that Adams and his colleagues wrote is as wide as the gulf between their morality and today's moral relativism. To his beloved wife, Abigail, Adams wrote at the beginning of their lives together, "I must entreat you, my dear Partner, in all the Joys and Sorrows, Prosperity and Adversity of my Life, to take a Part with me in the Struggle."

Their marriage lasted 54 years, and it is as much a paradigm for our time as are the documents to which Adams and the other founders pledged their lives, their fortunes and their sacred honor.

The conservative mind holds strongly to these principles and strives to pass them along to the next generation. It is not distracted by the appeal to fashions and trends. It does not seek the adulation of the *New York Times* or *Vanity Fair.* It understands that liberty and essential freedoms are a birthright that must be claimed by each new generation. It does not accept ideas like dialectical materialism and historical necessity that tempt tyrants and perpetuate dictatorships of the right and left. It does not place partisanship ahead of principle, or personal gain above the public good.

Above all, the conservative mind continually renews its own Declaration of Dependence on the grace of God. "Appeal to Heaven" was the phrase emblazoned on the colonists' flags. We hold aloft a similar flag today, raised for all of God's children, and pray, with the Psalmist, "Blessed is the nation whose God is the Lord, the people He chose for his inheritance." (Psalm 33:12).

Tony Perkins is President of the Washington, D.C.-based Family Research Council. He is a former member of the Louisiana legislature where he served for eight years, and he is recognized as a legislative pioneer for authoring measures like the nation's first Covenant Marriage law. Although he had no opposition for re-election, he kept his pledge to serve only two terms and left office at the completion of his term in 2004. He was a Republican candidate for the United States Senate in 2002. Since joining FRC in the fall of 2003 he has launched new initiatives to affirm and defend the Judeo-Christian values that this nation is founded upon.

Chuck Donovan, the Executive Vice President for Family Research Council, has more than three decades of experience in the national debates over the sanctity of life, family issues, and a wide range of other public policy topics. He manages the day-to-day operations of FRC and its staff of policy experts, communicators, government affairs specialists, as well as development, academic, and administrative professionals.

Mr. Donovan has written for himself and for many major public figures, and his writing has appeared in dozens of periodicals, including The Wall Street Journal, Reader's Digest, The New York Times, The Washington Post, The Weekly Standard, The Washington Times, The Cincinnati Enquirer, The San Diego Union, World Magazine, The American Library Journal, Citizen magazine of Focus on the Family, The National Catholic Register, American Legion magazine and dozens more.

# Commitment not Compromise

The conservative mind matters because the day we lose "in God we trust" would be an awful day.

The nations which have committed themselves to the God of Abraham, Isaac and Jacob have never followed Him perfectly. In fact, sometimes they followed Him very imperfectly.

This imperfection always brought rebuke from God, the rebuke taking many different forms.

But it is a completely different matter to decide that God will no longer be our God.

That is apostasy. That is ruin. That is disaster. Yet, that is what we have come to in the U.S.A.

Joshua, challenged the younger generation, when he was old and about to end his leadership. He challenged them to "choose you this day whom you will serve." And we now need to challenge our nation to choose, young and old.

Too many have wavered, waiting to see how the fight turns out. Too many have decided that they would let things happen in the comfort of their daily lives. Too many have thought they are powerless.

God has always helped the unable, but not the unwilling.

He helps the humble but not the hopeless.

He helps the faithful but not the fearful.

The result of conservative complacent inactivity is that our values have been hijacked and trashed by an active, vocal minority.

This minority has chosen to abandon God, declaring themselves to be athiests, or more commonly simply declaring that God is irrelevant. For them, God is unwanted in their personal lives. So, to them He is unwanted in the public square where our nation makes its decisions and debates its policies. And, they have forced the issue by continually chipping away at our expressions of God-ward commitment in court.

But the time has come for us to actively challenge this elitism, chauvinism and arrogant suppression of our nation's genuine godly heritage.

## The Conservative Mind is Important Because Freedom is not Free

All of us know the old adage that freedom is not free. And, of course it is not. It requires sacrifice and that sacrifice often includes our property, our sacred honor and even our lives. That is what the framers of our declaration of independence pledged.

But sacrifice is the result of a commitment. It does not flow from an attitude of entitlement.

Conservatives realize that we owe our country. We owe our family. We owe our neighbors. We owe, and we are therefore responsible.

But the people who would change our way of life focus on entitlement more than investment.

Virtually every court decision attacking our traditional family values has been supported by the complaint before the judge that "I'm entitled."

Virtually every court decision in favor of killing our children before their first breath has been urged because someone complained that "I'm the victim."

But victimhood and entitlement lead only to chains of immoral selfishness. They are incapable of leading to sacrifice. And since freedom is not free, they ultimately will lead to our enslavement by an all-encompassing government that compels obedience in the name of freedom.

## The Conservative Mind Matters Because it is not Always Politically Correct

I know that it isn't always politically correct to quote the Bible in our public discussions of politics and morals. We can quote the Koran, or the Dalai Lama. We can hold up various yogis or Bishop Tutu. We can even acknowledge that we believe that we ourselves are our own god, and that we need no salvation.

But to quote the Bible brings a shriek of shock: you have dared cross the one taboo in our society where nothing is taboo but the Bible.

But Washington quoted the Bible. So did Lincoln. So did both Roosevelts.

Jefferson himself even organized regular Christian worship in the public halls of congress. Imagine that.

It was the Bible thumpers who told our people that the King's authority was responsible to God and to the people, not merely something to which he was entitled by birth or conquest.

It was the Bible thumpers who sounded out the cry to destroy slavery.

It was the Bible thumpers who championed education for the poor.

It was the Bible thumpers who began our hospitals, our universities, our homes for the aged.

It was the Bible thumpers who said that the poor ought to be taken care of and that freedom ought to be spread around the world.

Can you imagine if the advocates of these needed changes to society had merely cited some vague notion of evolution, or the betterment of humanity? Without Bible thumping, the concept of equality would mean no more here than in modern China. Our leaders would loudly shout that we are all equal, only some are more equal than others.

In short, everything admirable that our society has done can be traced to leaders who not only believed the Bible, but who publicly thumped on it as the authority for their plans. Their commitment to God and His revealed word gave them power and gave them hope. They persevered in faith and because of that they were granted victory after moral victory.

But as surely as our leaders refuse to place their right hand on the Bible to enter office, their decisions will reflect the moral emptiness of their souls and the trivial selfish focus of their hearts. They will take the easy road of compromise when they should have stood on conviction.

## The conservative mind matters because we've got some folks on "the Hill" who just won't compromise

Believe it or not, we do have some people on Capitol Hill who will not compromise on things that they believe. It is popular and easy to be cynical about all politicians. And congress makes it easy. But the truth is that not everyone on the Hill is motivated by careerism and popularity.

Of course, everyone there is limited by the reality of politics. Politics has been described as "the art of the possible."

So, progress is slow. Sometimes it seems as if the people who are fighting for the right are accomplishing nothing. But that is only an appearance.

It is important to remember our history. When our soldiers were camped in Valley Forge, Washington had a very difficult time keeping the men from deserting.

Not only was the weather abominable, but the supplies were almost non-existent. Most of the soldiers could go home and resume their lives basically as they had before the war. Being farmers and shop owners, their daily lives changed little, whether the British or someone else was in charge.

But most disastrously for our Army was the impression, to the soldiers themselves, that nothing was happening. Washington realized that if he didn't do something then the army would fall apart. So he did something.

He brought in a mercenary Baron von Steuben who began to drill the troops.

The drilling helped two ways. It gave the troops something to do other than complain about the lack of activity. But, it also changed them from the rag-tag they were into a disciplined and organized fighting force. In other words, it changed how the men perceived themselves: fighters, not merely farmers, soldiers not merely shop-keepers.

Well, it is time for us to do something similar.

We have many conservative members of congress who are not willing to compromise or collapse at the first sign of opposition. In fact, many of them have been enduring the unending onslaught of criticisms from both their friends and their foes, and that for years. Yet they have neither given up the faith nor the fight.

We need to support them. We need to rally the troops. But in fact, we need to remind ourselves of just how much activity is actually happening. Then we need to commit ourselves to making more happen!

On January 21, 1776, Pastor John Muhlenberg preached from Ecclesiastes three. He focused on the eighth verse, which speaks about a time of war and a time for peace. He declared that this was the time of war. So, after prayer, standing in the pulpit, he took off the clerical robes, uncovering the Continental Army uniform he was wearing underneath! Over three hundred men joined him, to become the Eighth Virginia Brigade.

Pastors....can we do any less for the sake of God & patriotism in America?

May God bless us with the courage and the fervor we need!

### NO COMPROMISE

*The day we lose "in God we trust"*

*Would be an awful day,*

*Our nation was founded on this phrase*

*We'll let no one take that away.*

*"Under God" also seems*

*To be a great big threat,*

*But the USA will remain "Under God,"*

*For He has never failed us yet.*

*We will not bow, nor will we bend,*

*From the things that made us great,*

*We're patriotic, red-blooded Americans,*

*So let's just keep that straight.*

*We fight for right, what'er the cost,*

*And freedom is not free,*

*Abroad our troops have spilled their blood,*

*They did it for you and me.*

*America's still beautiful, she's still great,*

*We plan to keep it that way,*

*Tho not always "politically correct"*

*What does the Bible say?*

*That's our foundation, set in stone,*

*Some things just can't be changed,*

*We won't back down, nor recant,*

*But go forth in Jesus name.*

*We've got some folks up "On the hill"*

*Who just won't compromise,*

*They'll stand for right and the USA,*

*Until the day they die......*

*Poem written by Dr. Pearl Porter, May 20, 2008*

Dr. Pearl Porter was born into a sharecropper's family and raised in Alabama in a family of twelve. For the past twenty-six years she has pastored in Denver, and is the founder and director of Pearl Porter Ministries. She has ministered in churches around the country, along with radio and television. Dr. Porter is currently involved with building schools and churches in Costa Rica. Her most recent accomplishment is the founding of the Coalition of Patriotic Pastors and Leaders. She may be contacted at drpearlp@yahoo.com

# The Conservative Mind Blessed by God

**Fred Wehba**

Why does the conservative mind matter? Pat Williams, in an article entitled *Integrity is King*, listed ten universal characteristics of Integrity. Among the ten he listed were these six:

You know that little things count

You find the white when others see gray

You create a culture of trust

You care about the greater good

You hire integrity

You stay the course

I am convinced that there is no need to look further than Ronald Reagan and his transformational work as President to see why the conservative mind matters. His life reflected these points. But each conservative has his own story to tell and I cannot tell President Reagan's. So, by God's grace, I will bring you my own story, with its powerful material for understanding the importance of the conservative mind.

Ronald Reagan was often called "the Gipper." I won't go into how he came by this nickname. I think it is safe to say that most people don't know it's original reference. But, as an acronym it serves as a branding iron to burn into my mind what the conservative mind is and why it matters. Each letter reminds me of parts of my life. These images and experiences will powerfully affect you too.

## I — Integrity

Of course, the first letter in Gipper is G. But, being most important and obvious I will save that to the climax of this conversation.

"I" reminds me of the word integrity. Chuck Colson once said that "Integrity is the prime character quality that every individual needs above all." And he was not wrong! Integrity includes owning up to your situation, as well as dealing honestly even when it costs you heavily. Honesty and integrity are not merely words. To the conservative mind they make a dynamic difference in decision and action.

In 1985, I purchased *Athlete's Foot* and *Sports Spectrum*, with stores in the Galleria shopping centers in Dallas, Houston and Phoenix. I sold those stores in 1987. Then, in 1989 I purchased Los Angeles based *United Concrete Pipe Company*, for sixty million dollars, which led to our moving to Beverly Hills. The Lord tested my integrity time and again and reinforced its importance.

I later sold the company itself after I had sold the Los Angeles real estate part of it in 1992. But, it was anything but profitable. For one thing, because I had spent three years trying to operate this company, my real estate company became stagnant.

And, as if that weren't enough, I lost a considerable amount of money in the *UPCP*. I had some creditors from past real estate dealings. I even had problems stemming from *The Athlete's Foot* company.

One of the largest issues I faced was with the *Pension Benefit Guaranty Corporation (PBGC)*, which is part of the federal government. They accused me of owing over seventeen million dollars in underfunded pension liability for the employees of *United Concrete Pipe*. But, in fact, I did not owe this money. When I purchased it, we started a new pension plan for the employees, and as such I did not assume the underfunding problem from the previous owner.

However, I was told by an attorney that I should personally file bankruptcy to be rid of all of these claims. So, in the early months of 1993 I filed bankruptcy. This was the biggest mistake of my life.

I went through some very hard times. After a year, I decided to pay the creditors with a payout program and I paid all of them within twenty-four months. I was in the bankruptcy court for eighteen months.

This was a heartbreaking and humbling situation for me, especially since I had to start all over and had nothing to show for all I have done in the past. But the truth is that integrity is not always cheap. The conservative mind does not take the easy way out, and this is one of the primary reasons that the conservative mind matters.

## P — Perseverance

I attended my first year of college at North Texas State University in Denton, after which I transferred to the University of Oklahoma in Norman for my second year. Then for my third and fourth years I went back again to North Texas State.

I left college after my fourth year and went back home to Crowell, Texas for about two months. Following that, I went to Wellston, Oklahoma to work for my brother in his store. My work with him was very satisfying; to this day I have many great memories of that time. Then, in the fall of 1969 my father purchased a small grocery store in Oklahoma City.

I remember Dad purchased it for ten thousand dollars. I moved to Oklahoma City from Wellston and ran the store with my father who moved from Crowell a few months later. I worked very hard to promote that little store. With little or no money, I put up wood paneled walls that I purchased at salvage. I re-painted the store, used car wax to shine all of the refrigeration equipment: things such as the produce cases, meat cases, the frozen food and dairy cases. I fondly remember that new experience; I had great fun with it, although I worked every Saturday night mopping and waxing the floors. And I was tired each and every Saturday night. But quitting did not even enter my mind.

In 1971, I sold the store for fifty five thousand dollars. My father could not believe his eyes when I gave him the check. And, of course, he immediately purchased another store that was having problems. It had never been successful, so he bought it for nineteen thousand dollars. And I began again; I cleaned, scrubbed and did everything I knew to build this business. My many hours and perseverance finally let to the sale of this one for seventy five thousand dollars in 1976.

Finally, through perseverance, we were able to open my dream store, the details of which I will get to in a moment. But through all of the glamour of putting together our dream, we had a real problem, one that tested my perseverance to the limit. Three weeks before we were to open, *Kimbell & Co.*, our grocery supplier, sold out to *Winn Dixie*. *Kimbell* had guaranteed us inventory financing for five hundred thousand dollars at our bank. But *Winn Dixie* informed us that they would not honor *Kimbell's* commitment. We were about to open, and our financing vanished. I called the local grocery supplier, *Scrivner Wholesale Groceries* to meet with them. They gave me financing for one hundred sixty thousand dollars which was fully three hundred forty thousand short of what we needed. The store was programmed to lose one hundred fifty thousand in pre-opening costs and then eventually start making about thirty thousand per month.

But with our financing problems, after nine months I had to meet with an attorney. I asked him if we could meet with all of our suppliers to establish a payout to all of the vendors. We wanted to give them our financial statements to establish that we were profitable, but we had started without our full financing; nonetheless we could pay them out over the next year.

The attorney said that there was a mechanism in the court which was called Chapter Eleven, and through it I could pay all of my vendors in one year or even longer if needed. This seemed like a good thing. But I did not realize at the time that this was part of the bankruptcy court and potentially very harmful to my business reputation. Within a few days a receiver was appointed.

But, the storm had yet to reach maturity. There was no "debtor in possession" in those years. So, the receiver told me after the first week that he had received over four phone calls to sell the store. He himself was sixty-nine years old, couldn't be bothered, so he was going to sell the store.

He sold the store within a very short time. My father, my brother and I lost everything. It was hard on us, and very hard on our wives, especially my mother.

I wept in my car many times, many days.

Yet, after about four months, my former produce manager called me, asking if I would be interested in moving to Denver. I said "yes" and became Executive Vice President and Chief

Operating Officer of *Miller Supers. Miller's* was a local chain with sixteen stores. It had some real problems. I re-merchandised the stores. We then carried a much wider variety and increased the volume considerably. Finally, I helped them sell the stores. This was all in about two years, two years of perseverance on top of tremendous disappointment. But even in those times my life was spared by God's blessings and memorable moments.

## P — Play

The conservative mind is sometimes thought of as all work and little play. And, as I have related to you, work is very much a part of it. But the conservative mind also involves quite a bit of playfulness and pleasure. Quite frankly, I am convinced that no one can enjoy the fun and playfulness of life if they have little experience with long hard work to contrast it. The conservative mind involves humor, irony and many a practical joke. Sometimes the joke was on me.

I often think about the wonderful childhood I had in Crowell, Texas, and can remember when I first started working in my father's grocery store. I really tried to make it something special. I even painted the front of the store while he was away.

I went across the street to the Lumber Yard where Travis Vecera was working. Under his guidance, I purchased a supposedly burgundy paint to match the front of the store. After doing all the work to apply the paint, much more work in those days than now, I noticed that the color was actually "hot pink."

I went back to the lumber yard to complain, but Travis said that the paint would get darker when it dried.

It didn't.

Of course, my dad was out of town. I kept wanting to make myself like this color but I just couldn't. And when he returned, neither did Dad. I remember Dad going through the roof when he saw the pink. He hired our local painter, Gus Russell to paint the front of the store a light grey. Ultimately, it came off very nice, but I will never forget this incident.

I think Travis knew all along about the paint color. I'm sure he must had a great time laughing about it. And, I actually remember it myself with a wry smile from time to time.

## E — Experiment

Another misconception that the Gipper laid to rest is the conceit that the conservative mind is bent on maintaining the status quo. Quite the opposite. It is bent on building, improving, growing and perfecting. And these are based on trying. These are based on experimenting. I have mentioned above that I had worked at a failing store, turning it around to profitability, which led to my selling it for seventy five thousand dollars in 1976. All the while I was building up that troubled store, I was also working to arrange financing to enable me to build my dream store (which ended in Chapter Eleven, as I have already described). I will not reiterate those problems, but rather, I want to call your mind to another aspect of the conservative mind by telling what I omitted above.

I remember my brother telling my father and me, "why are you trying to get financing for four million dollars to build this store? We have no money and we are only making a small amount of money to support us."

Dad said "If he thinks he can do it then let's let him try."

I finally got the financing and we built this store. My brother and father both were equal partners with me. They sold their own stores as well, to become partners in this new one. This first class superstore had over fifty three thousand square feet with carpeting, suede wall coverings, a restaurant, a deli, a prime service meat counter, fresh fish, lobster, self-service meats, flowers, exotic produce, cookware, a bakery, a pharmacy, a cosmetic counter, *Godiva* chocolates, *Hallmark* greeting cards and food from all over the world. We also built a shopping center attached to the store. I remember Dad telling me what was being said when we had a pre-opening party with the mayor and other dignitaries from Oklahoma City. These dignitaries were saying that I had an unbelievable amount of guts to pull this off. We were all so proud of this great store and it was a great success. The average weekly volume was around three hundred thousand dollars per week which would probably equate to over one point two million per week in today's dollars.

Although that experiment ended badly, as I described, I did not quit experimenting. God has put it in my heart, in my blood.

After I built up and helped sell *Miller's*, I moved to Dallas to purchase a restaurant. I had operated it for about six months, when I purchased an insulation company. I had a small number of employees and we installed insulation in home attics and did commercial installations. We insulated *Mary Kay's* warehouses with exposed white insulation. This company did pretty well. After about twenty four months, I sold this company and purchased *Timesaver Templates*. I only had about thirty thousand dollars, but I purchased it for one and a quarter million. The former owner carried part of the purchase price while I refinanced his building to give him the down payment. I operated this company for thirty months and built up the volume while automating it. I sold the company for three and a quarter million, making two million in profit.

Next, a gentleman by the name of Dennis Lord encouraged me to get into the real estate business. He suggested that I move to downtown Dallas and get an office. He said "Fred, you are a deal junkie like I am, and you would really be good in buying real estate, going from deal to deal." So I moved downtown and got an office, calling my company *Westgate Investments*. I could not believe that I had made that much money and God was so good to me. I worked hard but God's blessings were just unbelievable. I remember praising Him nearly every day for all that He had done for me.

## R — Responsible

God had blessed my experimenting, but He did not bless me merely because I was willing to launch out on faith. He blessed me because I also have long had the conservative mind-set of responsibility. Jesus said "He who is faithful in what is least is faithful also in much; and he who is unjust in what is least is unjust also in much." He also said "Well done, good and faithful servant; you were faithful over a few things, I will make you ruler over many things."

I started meeting with brokers and others, leading me to purchase a large plot of land on Highway 75 north of Dallas, in McKinney, Texas. I bought it for two million, with a partner, Jon Wilson from Austin. This was my first real estate deal. Jon had his bank finance the land and we both signed the note. We put in about two hundred thousand each. When we sold it about eight months later, it was for about four million. I made one million, and he made the same amount. I was very fortunate, so I bought another piece of land in McKinney with John. We sold it and made about five hundred thousand.

The Lord was blessing our experiments. He was blessing our responsibility. We were doing very well. I then met Norman Brinker of *Brinker International* (formerly *Chili's*) at our next door neighbor's home (Leo and Bobbi Fields) for brunch. Leo was vice-chairman of *Zale's* and even though he is twenty years my senior, we still talk monthly. He still goes to the office where he now owns an investment company. Over a period of twenty four months, Norman and I partnered land in McKinney and Denton, as well as two shopping centers and a warehouse in Dallas. We sold the land in McKinney. Norman Brinker's family trust bought the rest of the property in 1987.

In truth, this conservative mindset of responsibility is closely tied to all the other traits that make the conservative mind matter. And this aspect of my conservative mind began early in my life.

In 1963, when I was only sixteen years old, my father had eighty percent of his stomach removed. As a result he was unable to work for an extended time. My mother and I ran the grocery store. I would work up the advertisements for the *Foard County News*. I also talked to all of the local vendors about what items would be good to put in our newspaper ads. I always tried to figure out a way that would draw as many customers as possible, and also to reflect the best price in town. Of course it was very difficult to do this, especially on price, because we had a small store with relatively low volume. The plain fact was that we were not the town's low cost grocery store, nor did we have the best equipment. Yet being responsible I was always working to overcome these obstacles. God blessed my responsibility, and so now I come to the most important aspect of my conservative mind, and the real reason that the conservative mind matters.

## G — God

The truth is that I have not been telling my story. I have been telling His story in my person. God created each of us, and the conservative mind not only acknowledges this, but works to conserve, preserve, spread and glorify this fact.

I grew up in the Methodist church in Crowell, Texas. I remember listening, with my mother to Tennessee Ernie Ford sing wonderful hymns. I first sang a solo in the Methodist church when I was only thirteen years old. The name of the song was *Ivory Palaces*, and this was a song that Tennessee Ernie Ford had sung on his album.

In 1963, during the year when my father had his stomach surgery, Jerry Craft came to town. He was an evangelist from Fort Worth. Jerry held services at both the Methodist and Baptist churches, and was powerfully dynamic in his delivery. He was a youth pastor, to whom about fifty students responded over the one week revival, giving their life to the Lord. It was a joyous time, and about three days into the services, I too gave my life to the Lord. What a great experience it was for me. God simply worked great things in my early life. And as my conservative mind grew, in His providence he continued to work great things. Through these great things (including great trials) God brought out the integrity, perseverance, playfulness, experimentation and responsibility which are the conservative mind. But, unfortunately, for some time my mind was more on the great matters of my life and less on the Great God who gave me the strength to triumph.

Realizing this, finally, in 1996, about eighteen months after my bankruptcy was dismissed, I rededicated my life to the

Lord. I was listening to a series of tapes by Charles Stanley called *David* and those tapes changed my life. I had been saved when I was sixteen. I had drifted away from God. I decided that I would change my life and rededicate myself to God. It was amazing what happened after that.

And now I want to share with you the American Dream – created by God – using the conservative mind.

In the spring of 1970 I married a wonderful young lady named Susan Diane Swaydan. We now have been married for thirty eight and a half years. She has stayed by my side through all the good times and bad. She always encouraged me. She never doubted my ability to make something happen. God has truly been with her and I deeply thank God for her presence in my life.

My oldest son, Fred Jr., started working with me in 1993, after he had worked about a year for *Lehman Brothers*. Then my second son, Chad, started working with me in 1995, becoming responsible for all the accounting and legal work in our company. Each one had their own responsibilities in the company. We all worked very hard. My third son, Christian, worked for me in the summer of 1996, then went to college shortly thereafter. Some time later, he worked with me for another couple of years, and finally, in January 2007 he moved to Australia where he opened a motorcycle store. My fourth son, Cyle, is practicing to compete on the professional golf tour. He has been on a professional tour prior to this year. Hopefully, he will make the "big time." Fred Jr. is now Vice-Chairman of our company. Chad is also a partner and is attending UCLA to get his MBA, two days a week, while working in our company four days a week.

By God's blessings, my sons and I bought over fifty buildings throughout the United States. These properties were triple net, single tenant properties. That meant that many of the buildings were processing properties for banks like *Bank of America*, or warehouses that large corporations would occupy. Since they had long term leases, I was able to place a large first mortgage and then a second mortgage on the property with very little cash flow. I did this for about seven years and then in 2004, I saw that we had about nine hundred million dollars of triple net, single tenant properties. We had significantly paid down the first and second mortgages. The properties were much more profitable as real estate became more popular, escalating the rental for the properties. Suddenly, these properties were worth approximately one billion five hundred thousand dollars. We sold most of the triple net properties and reinvested the funds into high profile, trophy properties like *The Four Seasons* in Dallas, *The Watergate* in Washington, D.C., the two skyscrapers that make up *Prudential Plaza* in Chicago, *Bank of America's* skyscraper in Atlanta and many more. Of the ten tallest buildings in the United States, we own two of them. God has blessed us so much that we now have nearly three billion in properties all over the United States.

And finally, in all the blessing that God has bestowed on me I have become acutely aware of one thing that the conservative mind is not:

## The Conservative Mind is not Self Centered

The most important thing I see is that we have underestimated the power of Jesus Christ and the wonderful love He gives to us so that our hearts are changed. Our attitude should always reflect the Holy Spirit in us. Our hearts need to reflect the glory of Jesus of whom the Scriptures say: "he made himself poor so that we through his poverty might be rich."

To God be the glory. This is why the conservative mind matters.

C. Fred Wheba is an Eagle Scout with Gold Palms. He has served in various capacities including board positions for the following organizations: The Boy Scouts of America, California Baptist University, First Baptist Church of Beverly Hills, InChrist Church of Beverly Hills, The Church at Beverly Hills, Westside Community Church, The Institute for Social and Economic Policy on the Middle East, the Harvard University John F. Kennedy School of Government, The Dove Foundation, and the Associates for Breast Cancer Studies (ABC's) as a part of the John Wayne Cancer Institute, Cedars Sinai Board of Governors, Team Beverly Hills, Los Angeles World Affairs Council, The Beverly Hills Education Foundation. He is listed in *Who's Who of American Business Leaders*, is actively involved in more than thirty charities around the United States and has served in the creation, development and leadership of several Christian churches.

In 1990 he was recognized by Los Angeles Mayor Tom Bradley as Man of the Year. In 2003, Suzi and he were honored for charitable efforts with the Muscular Dystrophy Association's (MDA) Humanitarian Award. They were again acknowledged in 2004 by California Baptist University with the Spirit of Excellence award for achievements in philanthropic endeavors. In 2006 the Jeffrey Foundation honored both.

# Epilogue

This December of 2008, will mark the 20th anniversary of Give Me a Chance Ministry, which is now Education for All, an organization that helps students prepare to enter college through our Achiever Mentor Program. We provide information on college preparation, selection, and scholarships available through our organization, various non-profit organizations, and member colleges and universities.

Give Me a Chance Ministry was founded in 1988 to provide at-risk students who had a desire to attend college an avenue to enter a premiere university. Many of the students we served did not meet the rigorous academic standards of Oral Roberts University (ORU) but we were able to stand in the gap and ask the university to give them a chance. We placed no demands on the university, we simply asked them to help students who otherwise may not have a chance to receive a college education.

You see, I was an at-risk student who grew up during segregation and doubted my ability to go to college. This is why I felt compelled to begin an organization to help students gain entrance and matriculate from ORU, while I was a student in Seminary there. This program was successful and we were able to increase the black enrollment from 5 percent to 22.5 percent in four years. We provided tutoring, mentoring, and scholarships for many of our students. Our efforts were not only directed to black students; we helped at-risk students from all backgrounds and socio-economic states. We were able to assist Anglo students, Hispanics, American Indians, and international students, particularly from countries in the Caribbean. Many of these students are successful today because of the opportunity and access we afforded them through our partnership with Oral Roberts University. We are forever grateful to Oral Roberts for embracing our efforts and for giving students a chance to succeed.

Today, Education for All extends its program to include other universities, colleges, and technical schools. It is our goal to inspire, educate, and empower students through initiatives such as our Achievers Program. This program will encourage, teach, and mentor emerging achievers to build success on principles of virtue.

Education for All is proud of the new direction we have taken. For more information, please write us at P.O. Box 40949, Memphis, TN 38174. Our website www.edforall.com will be available soon. Please visit our site and support our efforts.

*Best wishes,*
*Bill and Deborah Owens*

# Why The Conservative Mind Matters

A Collection of Essays
from Bill Owens

In order to keep our prices low, you can only
order this book online.
For questions, please email us at:
online@highstandardpublishers.com

**Retail Price $14.95**

Discount Rates:

Order at:
www.theconservativemind.org

# Why The Conservative Mind Matters

## A Collaboration of Essays With Bill Owens

Book Discount Order Form

In order to keep our prices low, you can only order this book online.
For questions, please email us at:
orders@higherstandardpublishers.com

### Retail Price $16.95

Discount Rates
10-24      13.95 per book
25-49      11.95 per book
50-99       9.95 per book
100-199     7.95 per book

*For orders exceeeding 200 please call us at:*
*800-791-5806 ext 150*

## Order at:
## www.theconservativemind.org

*Shipping and handling will be determined at time of order.*